CW00347825

A LITTLE
BURNS LORE

COMPILED BY

JOHN D. ROSS, LL.D.

EDITOR OF "HIGHLAND MARY," "ROUND BURNS' GRAVE,"
"BURNSIANA," "BURNS' CLARINDA,"
"HENLEY AND BURNS," ETC.

WITH A PREFACE BY

JAMES D. LAW

AUTHOR OF "DREAMS O' HAME, AND OTHER POEMS," ETC.

LANG SYNE
PUBLISHING

Published by
LANG SYNE PUBLISHERS LTD

Printed by
DARNLEY PRESS LTD
Unit 1C, Whitecrook Centre,
78 Whitecrook Street,
Clydebank G81 1QS

PUBLISHER'S PREFACE TO
THE 1991 EDITION

For many years this treasure trove of fascinating facts, snippets and stories about the life of Robert Burns has been a rarity, eagerly sought after by Burns lovers on the shelves of the antiquarian bookseller. Now the classic "Little Book of Burns Lore", originally published by Eneas MacKay of Stirling in 1926, is reissued for the 1990s.

Discover why the ploughman genius who became our most famous poet was almost forced to flee to the West Indies in despair before most of his best work was written. The two loves of his life were devoted, loyal wife Jean Armour and the mysterious, tragic Highland Mary — but what kind of women were they and what influence did they have on the poet? How was a draper's bill for a few pounds, delivered to his death bed, the catalyst for false stories that he died in poverty? Why was he so sarcastic of Kirk ministers — "the lads in black" — and how did he force them to think again? What is the truth about Burns and drink? How did Freemasonry open doors to the rich and powerful? What are the many other "waifs and strays" from his life that will come as a surprise to many readers? All the answers are here.

The book also traces Burn's early days among the fishermen and smugglers of the Ayrshire coast. His vivid imagination was fired listening in the shielings to tales of pirates, ghosts and witches. Later he made the long walk to Edinburgh in search of fame and fortune. The poet lived in a slum but still managed to become the darling of capital society.

And the true stories and people behind his poems are recounted. A farmer's lie to his superstitious wife about a lost bonnet and purse was the inspiration for Tam O'Shanter. For Tam, Souter Johnny, the Lass o'Ballochmyle, Cutty Sark, Kirkton Jean and many other characters in his poems were based on real people who lived and worked in Ayrshire. Discover their true identities in these pages.

CONTENTS.

CONTENTS.

ROBERT BURNS is of perennial interest to all
students of Universal Literature, while to his own
people he remains a permanently paramount
figure both as a Poet and as a Person. New
editions of his writings are constantly appearing,
and several extensive Biographies of him have
recently been written and liberally reviewed.
The world in recent years has radically revised
its views of Burns on many important points
as new documents have come to light, or are
permitted to be published, and "Scotia's darling
bard" is now shown in a much fairer and truer
light than hitherto had been possible from the
mistakenly prejudiced concoctions of his con-
temporaries or even the wilfully biased compilations of later would-be authorities. We now have
an astonishingly complete collection of the writings
of Burns in prose and in verse, and almost every
year important and true items relating to his
life and habits are added to the meagre outlines
that first did duty as his personal history. His
MSS. and his first editions are steadily increasing
in value, and will continue to do so as sure as their
numbers are limited and our rich collectors become
more numerous. Even as I write these lines the
cable informs us that at a recent London auction
sale (April 8), a Philadelphia dealer paid £1,750
for a fine specimen of the Kilmarnock Burns. As
is well known, the Poet made his initial appearance

in book form *via* the subscription route, his
objective at the time being less poetic fame than
passage money to waft him to Jamaica, where
he had secured a situation as a plantation overseer.
Probably had Burns got thus far he would have
sooner or later joined many of his countrymen in
the new United States of America, but Fate inter-
vened, and Fortune kept him back to dree his
weird at home. His total profits from the first
edition did not much exceed twenty pounds, and
his local printer would not assume the risk of a
second impression. Several subscribers to the
first edition repented of their bargain when the
book was ready for delivery, and on the only list
now known to be extant, against the name of such
a welcher (one " Lorimer ") Burns himself wrote,
" The blockhead refused it." Perhaps that very
volume is the one recently sold at the Kilmarnock
record price—for the time being.

The present Miscellany by Dr. Ross is an interesting addition to his imposing library of Burnsiana,
making the twenty-third complete volume from
the pen of this painstaking editor and authority
on all that relates to his admired and beloved
compatriot. The very titles of his compilations
are alluring, and the varied items in their total
bulk constitute a most fascinating anthology of
valuable contributions, featuring episodes and
out-of-the-way information authentically associated with the life and writings of Burns. No other

collector on either side of the Atlantic has been so prolific in his garnerings of personalia; no other Burns scholar anywhere has given us such a series of humanly critical compendiums, and all lovers of Burns, and indeed of Scottish literature generally, owe a distinct debt of gratitude to Dr. Ross for the convenient preservation of many "waifs and strays" that otherwise might be difficult to locate, scattered as they are in magazines, newspapers, and private repositories. In this connection, I am very hopeful that the present volume will be successful from the publisher's point of view, and that it may prove to be the initial or forerunner of a series of similar "Little Books of Burns Lore."

JAMES D. LAW.

ROXBOROUGH,
PHILADELPHIA, PA., U.S.A.,
April, 1925.

A LITTLE BOOK OF
BURNS LORE.

THE BIRTHDAY OF BURNS.

UNIQUE is the glory which his admiring countrymen and their descendants shower on the memory
of the Scottish ploughman-poet. To what man of
letters, national bard or otherwise, of the present
or of an age remote, does his race, of near kin or
far, pay such constant and unqualified devotion
as Scotsmen do to the bard of Ayr, particularly
on his every birthday anniversary, the 25th of
January? Universal is the homage with which
they reward his genius, for in every town and
city throughout the broad earth a company of
Scots, large or small, gathers on that day to do him
honour in feast and dance and song. Unstinted
is the love—a broad love, too, unlike, in this, the
national characteristic, which is so illustrative of
Kipling's line :

Ye are sons of the blood, less sure to bless than to ban—

which they bear him, for woe to the critic who dares,
in any Scottish company, to point to or even to
hint at any of the human weaknesses by which
the life of "rantin', rovin' Robin" was beset.

The anniversary of the birth of Robert Burns is the red letter day in the Scottish calendar at home and abroad. What would have been the thoughts of the brilliant, happy-dispositioned, sensitive-minded, intensely emotional, mirth-loving, honest and independent young Scotsman of the " auld toon of Ayr," who brought his countrymen of culture and of care to his feet by his greatest ambition.

> For puir auld Scotland's sake,
> To sing a sang, at least,

had he dreamed that a century after his death his name would be sounded with praise akin to worship in almost every hamlet on the globe ? Little did he think, although he himself prophesied that he would " be better appreciated a hundred years hence," that on the wings of the four winds of the earth his name and fame would be borne over the seas to the uttermost ends, and that the tributes of his own loved native land would be echoed in the depths of the African forest, from the plains of Australia, on India's coral strand, and would ring back with a wild enthusiasm from the hills and valleys of the western world, to which at one time he almost came, even to the confines of the pole, where the miners in the Klondike will gather round the campfire and make the frozen regions of the great and solemn Northwest ring with the melodies of the songs which sprang from his mind and heart ?

Stately mausoleums have been erected in many places to commemorate his life and work and personality, and innumerable statues, the finest examples of the sculptors' art, have been set up all over the world, but this constantly swelling pean of the universal admiration and love of his countrymen and of the world is the greatest monument of them all.

Perhaps the fact that the life of Burns was full of hardships and disappointments, and that his genius and personality were triumphant over the coldness of a local world that, with a most remarkable agility, recognised his talent, but at the same time turned a frigid shoulder toward his efforts to lift himself into a better material state, is a reason for this remarkable adoration. He had been kicked and cuffed, and keenly did his ultra-sensitive nature suffer from the plots and attacks of his enemies, toward whom he rarely if ever turned in the spirit of compromise. To suffer and to smile—to grin and bear it—is one of the sure ways for a Scot to win the admiration of his fellows. Burns kept on smiling amid his misfortunes, and, more, he kept on singing. And it did not come to him in any literal way to practise the injunction regarding the turning of the other cheek. Instead, he employed his pen in the making of some of the most scathing examples of sarcastic verse which the language has ever been employed to build. Who can tell how much the

B

terrible satire which Burns penned under the title
of "Holy Willie's Prayer" helped to lift the
Scottish kirk from its old time narrowness ?

The tenderness of the humanity of Burns is
shown in his verses "To a Mouse" and "To a
Mountain Daisy," which were composed while
the poet was at the plough. "I could point out,"
wrote his brother Gilbert, "the particular spot
where each was composed. Holding the plow
was a favourite situation with Robert for poetic
compositions, and some of his best verses were
produced while he was at that exercise."

The beauty of the love songs which Burns gave
to the world is of a grade which has been surpassed
by no writer in any age. "Afton Water," an
apostrophe to that beautiful river, written upon
the Coitsfield dairymaid, the dearly beloved and
long remembered Highland Mary, saddens with
its wonderful cadence the most prosaic of mortals,
and with its incomparable gentle sorrowing soothes
the surging of the stormiest heart :

> Flow gently, sweet Afton, among thy green braes,
> Flow gently, I'll sing thee a song in thy praise ;
> My Mary's asleep by thy murmuring stream—
> Flow gently, sweet Afton, disturb not her dream.
>
> Thou stock-dove, whose echo resounds through the
>   glen,
> Ye wild whistling blackbirds in yon thorny den,
> Thou green crested lapwing, thy screaming forbear—
> I charge you disturb not my slumbering fair.

And the charming classic " O' a' the Airts,"
written in honour of his wife, Jean Armour, while
alone at lovely Ellisland building a home for her
and for their children, is a touching proof of the
fact that, though it had passed through many a
fiery ordeal, his heart was still full of tenderness
for her who was his first love, and whose devotion
through good report and ill never allowed a murmur
to escape her lips.

> O' a' the airts the wind can blaw,
>   I dearly like the West,
> For there the bonny lassie lives,
>   The lassie I love best.
> There wild woods grow, and rivers row,
>   And mony a hill between,
> But day and night, my fancy's flight
>   Is ever wi' my Jean.

Through the hundred years and over which have
sunk into oblivion since this most remarkable
singer gave to the world a series of lyrics and poems
which have made his fame an eternal endurance
and his personality beloved beyond that of any
other in the world's history, his influence has
grown like the mustard seed. His countrymen
have marched to battle and to death with a magni-
ficence of fearlessness born of the strains of " Scots
Wha Hae," a song which, to quote Carlyle, should
be sung with the voice of a whirlwind. (And
Burns was one of the very few, by the way, over
whom Carlyle did not ride rough shod.) The

pathos of " Man Was Made to Mourn " has softened
many a miser's and tyrant's heart, and the stirring,
rugged lines of " A Man's a Man for a' That " have
spurred on many a wearied life to high and noble
effort and the achievement of heroic independence.
He struck the chords of the national heart, touching
the keys here and there with surpassing effect
by the mere mention of Scotland's hill and dales
and streams, dashing the colour with ingenuous
manipulation on the pictures of national customs
and character, working in the shade and tint
with a truthfulness which will stand the wear and
tear of time. The influence of his democratic
spirit has played no small part in the building up
of the sentiments which have made our beloved
western land the safe and abiding home of Freedom.
It is no wonder, then, that Scotsmen honour the
memory of Robert Burns, and no wonder that the
name of the humble Scottish singer has become
a household word wherever the Anglo-Saxon
tongue is spoken and sung.

DAVID DUNCAN FLETCHER.

BURNS AND HIS LOVE OF BOOKS.

THE diffusion of knowledge was a favourite object
with Burns. For this he established his reading
and debating clubs in the west, and in the same
spirit he desired to excite a love of literature among
the peasants of Dunscore. He undertook the

management of a small parochial library, and wrote out the rules. Mr. Riddell, of Friars-Carse, and other gentlemen, contributed money and books. The library commenced briskly, but soon languished. The poet could not always be present at the meetings; the subscribers lived far apart; disputes and disunion crept in, and it died away like a flower which fades for want of watering. Burns alludes ironically to the scheme in one of his letters. "Wisdom," he averred, " might be gained by the mere handling of books." His letters to the booksellers on the subject of this subscription library do him much honour; his choice of authors, which business was actually left to his discretion, being in the highest degree judicious.

Such institutions are now common, indeed almost universal, in the rural districts of Southern Scotland, but it should never be forgotten that Burns was among the first, if not the very first, to set the example. " He was so good," says Mr. Riddell, " as to take the whole management of this concern; he was treasurer, librarian, and censor, to our little society, which will long have a grateful sense of his public spirit and exertions for its improvement and information.

COLIN RAE BROWN.

COLIN RAE BROWN was born at Greenock, August

19, 1821, and died at London, September 11, 1897. He was a man of most engaging manners, and was held in high esteem by every one who knew him. "He contributed," says the *Burns Chronicle* for 1898, "both in prose and poetry to the leading periodicals of the day, and his Burns enthusiasm was such that, for half a century he was the head and front of every movement in honour of the National Bard. For many years he was honorary secretary of the Greenock Burns' Club, and he was closely associated with Professor Wilson ('Christopher North') in organising the great Ayr Festival of 1844. . . . . It was in the columns of the *Bulletin* that he made his first appeal to Scotsmen for the erection of the Wallace Monument, and when, mainly through his advocacy, the movement took practical shape, he was appointed convener and chairman of the permanent executive committee. In conjunction with Sir Archibald Alison, Sheriff Glassford Bell, Professor Nichol, and other representative Scotsmen, he organised the Burns Centenary Festival of 1859, and it was greatly owing to his characteristic energy that that event was such a memorable success. He was one of the founders of the Burns Federation, of which body he had been an honorary vice-president since its foundation in 1885. It was also on his suggestion that the Federation undertook the publication of the *Burns Chronicle*, for the success of which he evinced the most lively concern down to the day of his death. When the centenary of the publication of the First Edition was celebrated in Kilmarnock in 1886, as the representative of the London Burns Club he was the honoured guest of the brilliant array of the talent of the West which that occasion brought together. Among his personal friends were De Quincey, Samuel Lover, and Colonel Glencairn Burns, the youngest surviving son of the Poet. Mr. Rae Brown occupies a high position among our recent minor poets. In his early years he published 'Lays and Lyrics by Sea and Land,' and more recently, 'Noble Love' and 'The Dawn of Love,' all of which have had an extensive circulation."

A HUNDRED YEARS.

1796-1896.

A HUNDRED YEARS ! yet the glorious throne
Of Scottish Song is still thine own—
A type of the Centuries waiting thee,
Who sang the Charter of the Free !

Hustling the living and trampling the dead,
The years rush on with resistless tread—
Crowns and Kingdoms may disappear,
But Time ever yieldeth another year.

Humble the bed that gave thee birth :
Lowly as that from which—from Earth—
Thy spirit leaped, strong in its faith,
And sought the friendly arms of Death.

Strong in its faith ! faith in a World,
Repentant, that so long had hurled
Its dire damnation on the head
Soon number'd with the mighty Dead.

Then, like a dazzling Splendour came
That Worship of thy name and fame—
To scorch Detraction's lying tongue,
As forth Truth's golden joy-bells rung !

A Hundred Years ! how swift their flight !
From darkness to unclouded light—
To where thy Fame's perennial Sun
Its endless course hath but begun !

With silence, then, shall the toast be met
Of " The Bard " whose sun shall never set—
Flashing its glory from shore to shore,
A joy of the world for evermore—?

With *silence ?* no ! or said or sung,
Thy name shall lie on ev'ry tongue,
And in the hearts of all mankind
The deathless fame of BURNS enshrined !

COLIN RAE BROWN.

BURNSIANA.

IN Wood's edition of the Songs of Scotland,
published in 1849, there appeared the following
reminiscences of Burns, by Miss Logan of Cumnock,
obtained by the editor, Mr. Graham, through the
Rev. James Murray, then minister of the parish :—

"RECOLLECTIONS OF BURNS, BY MISS JANET
LOGAN, OF CUMNOCK, DAUGHTER OF HUGH
LOGAN, ESQ., OF THAT ILK.

"Remembers having met with Robert Burns the poet, about sixty years ago, in the house of Mrs. Merry, Old Cumnock. He had not then visited Edinburgh, but was farmer of Mossgiel, in the neighbourhood of Mauchline. Mrs. Merry was youngest daughter of Mr. Rankine of Adamhill, whom Burns in one of his productions describes as 'Rough, rude, and ready-witted.' Mrs. Merry was well known to be the heroine of 'The Lea-rig.' Some say it was another person, but it was not so. Remembers Mrs. Merry's having told her that Burns, when he visited her father's house for the first time, on being shown into a room, went round a piece of carpet which only partially covered the floor—as was usual in those times—as if afraid of setting foot upon it; but whether he did so by way of sly burlesque, or really from the notion that such things were intended only for his *betters*, does not know. Remembers, on the occasion above referred to, seeing Burns walking about the streets of Cumnock with Walter Morton, the excise-officer of the place. Remembers, that when Burns and Morton came in with others who were to meet with them, Mrs. Merry remarked to him, by way of joke, that all the *yill-wives* of Cumnock had been put nearly beside themselves at his appearance with Morton—thinking him the supervisor. Remembers Burns turning round to his companion, and exclaiming, rather more warmly than the occasion seemed to require, 'That *I* should be mistaken

for one of your—set ! ' Does not remember any of
Burns' remarks during the evening. Thinks of
the conversation as chiefly of a political nature.
Remembers that Burns was very animated, and
apparently in high spirits. Has been at many
rockings, or parties of a similar kind, and has had
many opportunities of marking the manners of
those with whom the poet at that time associated.
Thinks that his manners and behaviour were not
superior to those of his compeers. Is rather of
opinion that he was somewhat coarse in his
behaviour, and boisterous in his address. Remembers that he wore his hair tied—was good
looking—thick-set—not very tall. Has heard that
he played the violin, but never was present when
he played on that instrument. Never heard him
sing.   (Signed)   'JANET LOGAN.' "
    The editor appended the following note :—
    The editor of this work, when thanking the Rev.
Mr. Murray and Miss Logan for the above com-
munication, made the following observations in
his letter of 13th June, 1849 :—" I mentioned to
you that the only person I know now, who was
well acquainted with Burns, is my mother. I
told you of Burns' offer to write to her a journal
of his Highland tour, and of her hesitation to accept
his offer, without the concurrence of her father
and mother. Burns' pride was hurt by that
hesitation, and he never renewed the offer, and
never wrote a line to her afterwards. Burns

was a very frequent guest at my grandfather's house in Edinburgh, during Burns' residence there ; and it was in that way that he became acquainted with my mother, who was then a young unmarried woman, and who certainly could not with propriety accept of Burns' offer of letter-writing, without the sanction of her parents. Burns must, at that time, have received some polish of manner from his intercourse with Edinburgh society ; for my mother describes him as a man who conducted himself with perfect propriety amongst his superiors in *social* position. It is easy to imagine how quickly a man of Burns' tact and shrewd observation would adapt himself to the manners of his friends in the metropolis of Scotland so far as matters of mere *etiquette* went." The editor's mother has often spoken to him of Burns' remarkable conversational powers. She has also told him that no one of the portraits of Burns that she has seen—nor even the one by Skirving—gives an idea of the extraordinary fire and expression of Burns' eyes.

BURNS' ANCESTORS.

IN a sunless, sleepy little hollow in the agricultural county of Kincardine is a graveyard which is annually visited by many Scotsmen who worship at the shrine of Robert Burns. In Glenbervie Kirkyard, the lonely burying ground referred to, is the dust of several connecting links between Scotland's bard and the northern home of his father ; and in June of 1885, in connection therewith, a ceremony of national importance took place. That was the handing over to the parish heritors of two renovated tombstones which were found about fifty years ago in a dilapidated condition, broken and weather-corroded, lying among the long grass of the old kirkyard. One of the stones had originally been erected about 150 years ago, and the other about thirty years previously, over the graves of members of the Burness family, who tilled the ground in the immediate neighbourhood. For well-nigh 200 years after those farmers of the Mearns were laid to their rest, men and women passed by the tombstones with only a fleeting thought of the men whose names were inscribed thereon. Time passed. William Burness, the son of the farmer of Clochinhill, near Stonehaven, left his paternal home to fight his own battle with the world. Edinburgh was then the Mecca of Scottish gardeners, and he made his way south to the capital. From Edinburgh he passed to Ayrshire, and there he and his wife made their home in the " auld clay biggin' " where their son Robert Burns was born. Then Scotland and Scottish patriotism had a mouthpiece, and the whence of Robert Burns' family was a subject discussed by eminent genealogists and litterateurs.

The poet sang and passed away, but his memory lived. The graves of his ancestors were visited, the neglected and broken tombstones discovered and renovated, and the fact of their presence made known to an interested world. The inscriptions on the restored tombstones sufficiently describe their origin and restoration :—

1. In memory of James Burnes, tenant in Brawlinmuir, died 23rd January, 1746. Margaret Falconer, his wife, died 28th December, 1749. This tomb of the great grand-parents of the poet Robert Burns, restored by subscription, 1885.

2. In memory of William Burnes, tenant in Bogjorgan, who died, 1715 ; and Christian Fotheringham, his wife. This tomb of the great grand-uncle of the poet Robert Burns, restored by subscription, 1885.

THE ADVENTURES OF A " KILMARNOCK BURNS."

PROBABLY no book in the literary history of Scotland has, as a mere book, had a more romantic career than this volume, which contains the first-fruits of its greatest man of genius. A thin octavo in form, it was issued, poorly printed on poor paper, in 1786, from the press of its printer, John Wilson of Kilmarnock, at the humble price of three shillings. Six hundred copies were printed and bound in boards, white as to the back, and bluish-gray as to the sides. In a month not a copy remained unsold—it is doubtful, indeed, if the poet himself got a copy—and the author's capital was recruited to the extent of £20 ; not a bad return. Notwithstanding the success of the venture, so poor an opinion had Wilson of the volume that he declined to entertain the idea of a second edition, unless Burns could defray the cost of the paper to print it on—namely, £27. This was simply impossible for the man into whose pouch the deil had entered once for all, and so the poet bade auld Killie farewell as an author. It was then that Burns, disheartened at his prospects, took his chest as far as Greenock, on his way to the West Indies ; but here Dr. Blacklock, through Burns' friend Lawrie, stepped in with proposals for the first Edinburgh edition, which finally stopped his migration ; and before the beginning of 1787 Creech was advertising the first Edinburgh edition, which had an immense list of subscribers, and was quickly followed by another, hardly less successful. It is now believed that, both as regards the number of editions and the aggregate sale, the *Poems* of Burns stand only below the Bible and Shakespeare. About fifty years ago (1846) a somewhat unaccountable rise took place in the value of the Kilmarnock Burns. I suppose the cause may be looked for in the rise of the American book-collector, and the comparative scarcity of the volume, many copies having, from much handling, been worn out of existence. The Kilmarnock Burns was described in an early bibliographical book of Mr. Slater's as "perhaps for its size the most valuable book in existence."

As when this was written the market price for a copy was about £120, I have often wondered in what terms Mr. Slater would describe it now that it has changed hands, as it did the other day at Paisley, for £1,000. When I was in the book trade in the city of London, about thirty years ago, I had an adventure with a copy which may amuse your readers. Among my customers was a Scotsman, a native of Dundee, but then in business in Whitechapel. He was not a man of much culture, but he had, I believe, been smitten by the late Mr. Lamb of Dundee with the craze for the collection of rare books. Mr. Lamb had himself a very fine copy of the Kilmarnock Burns, nearly perfect, which at his sale brought some £575. This is the second highest price the volume had yet fetched at auction, and it was whispered that the price, which was then abnormal, arose entirely from the fact of two dealers bidding against each other in the interests of the same American client.

To resume my story, my customer one day expressed a strong desire to have a copy of the Kilmarnock Burns. When I asked him what price he would give, he promptly responded £50. On this basis I set to work, and at last heard of a copy in the hands of an Edinburgh bookseller. When I asked him his price, he said £25 ; but, when he sent for it on my inspection, he was so honourable as to point out that the last leaf of the glossary appeared to be in facsimile, and the price would in consequence be reduced to £20. It was a poor copy, bound in contemporary calf, probably a presentation copy. I at once waited with it on my customer. I did not see any reason why I should abate the price to him, but I was careful to point out to him the doubtful leaf. He, however, was hardly a man to appreciate such a technical point as that, and so he cheerfully drew me a cheque for £50.

About a month after his purchase my client waited on me to say that he was sorry he could not keep that copy, as the thought of that leaf kept him awake o' nights. He therefore resolved to sell it, and I might look out for a better one. He possessed some small pieces in Burns' handwriting, and one of these he inserted under the front board of the volume as a sort of *bonne-bouche*. He then sent it to Messrs. Puttick & Simpson's saleroom, where it fetched £75 !

JAMES DRUMMOND (in 1906).

THE " AULD BRIG " OF AYR.

TRADITION is uncertain concerning the exact date of the " auld brig." Some authorities locate its origin about 1232, while others make it younger by a century and a half. Six centuries at least look out upon the visitor from its mediæval arches. To Burns, however, the romance associated with the bridge is due. In 1786 the bard was part-tenant of Mossgiel, thirteen miles west of Ayr. He was floundering in the trough of the sea economically, yet overhead his star of genius was fast rising towards Fame's zenith. In August of that wonderful Burnsian year his first volume of poems was published by John Wilson, in Kilmarnock ; but the book did not contain the poem of " The Brigs of Ayr," which appeared for the first time in the second and Edinburgh edition in April, 1787.

The county town of Ayr had two market-days in the week—Tuesday and Friday. Burns was frequently in Ayr on business, and Friday, apparently, was his favourite day. He would drive to market in the farm-cart, or ride. Chief among his numerous friends in Ayr were Robert Aiken— " My lov'd, my honour'd, much respected friend ! " —to whom " The Cottar's Saturday Night " was inscribed—and John Ballantyne, to whom the like compliment was paid in " The Brig of Ayr." Ballantyne was a banker, and was Provost of the Burgh in 1786. Aiken was a writer ; both were

foremost among townsmen. The earliest reference
to " The Brigs of Ayr " occurs in a letter to Aiken,
dated mysteriously, "Ayrshire, 1786," and written
manifestly when Burns was in hiding, that is to
say, about September, in which he remarks thus :—
" There is scarcely anything hurts me so much in
being disappointed of my second edition as not
having it in my power to show my gratitude to
Mr. Ballantyne by publishing my poem of ' The
Brigs of Ayr.' "   Burns had failed to arrange with
the undiscerning Wilson for a second edition,
notwithstanding an offer from Ballantyne of £27
towards expenses.

The poem, therefore, which has conferred a
world's name upon the " auld brig " must have
been composed very early in the autumn of 1786.
When wandering in Ayrshire, keeping out of the
way of the Armours, anxious about the future, a
love-lorn swain, the poet would be much in Ayr.
He had spent a night in the town, and dreamt
himself into the fantasy of the poem, probably
after returning from a midnight ramble by the
river, and in sight of the contrast between the
" auld brig " and the coming new one.   In fancy
he sees " two dusky forms dart through the midnight air," and alight opposite each other—the
one on the " auld brig," the other on the " rising
piers " of its rival about to be.   These " Sprites "
derived their features from the architecture of
the bridges ; " auld brig appeared o' ancient

Pictish race, the vera wrinkles Gothic in his face ; "
whereas " new brig was buskit in a braw new coat,
that he at Lon'on frae ane Adams got." There-
upon the " Sprites " of the two bridges engage in a
duel in verse, which in point of tone and manner
is reminiscent somewhat of the " flyting " of old
days between such Scotch vernacular poets as
Dunbar and Kennedy. It is modernity pitted
against antiquity in a tourney of wit ; the
embryonic commercialism of Scotland in the
last quarter of the eighteenth century against
the old, slow-sure soporific methods of the then
departing ages ; the pride of years against the
conceit of youth. In course of the " flyting,"
the " auld brig " dares to utter the famous
prophecy :—" I'll be a brig when ye're a shapeless
cairn," which came true in 1877, when Provost
Ballantyne's new bridge of 1785-88, then ninety
years old, fell to pieces, and was superseded by the
existing masonry.

In " The Brigs of Ayr " the fertility of Burns'
fancy during the grand creative period of his muse
at Mossgiel is illustrated. The poet fights on both
sides—for the old and for the new—with almost
equal deftness of stroke, albeit there are traces of
prejudice in favour of the " auld brig," which reveal
the conservatism of the intellect and the heart
inherent in Burns' mixed pyschologic endowment.
By the ultimate destruction of the new bridge in
an exceptionally heavy thaw-flood, it would be

demonstrated that " architecture's noble art was
lost ; " yet this impeachment of a superficial
modernity is answered by an equally realistic
sketch of the forbidding features of Gothic architecture :—" Gaunt,   ghastly,   ghaist-alluring
edifices, hanging with threatening jut, like preci-
pices." At length the " flyting " was interrupted
by " a fairy train dancing down the glittering
stream," attended by minstrels and bards, in front
the venerable genius of the stream crowned with
water-lilies, the throng being followed by figures
that personify the circle of the poet's loves—
Female Beauty, The Seasons, Courage, Learning
and Worth, and Peace. At sight of these jocund
and beneficent fairies, the " Sprites forgot their
kindling wrath."

From the technical point of view, this poem,
written in rhymed heroics, discovers the influence
of Pope and Shenstone upon Burns, not less than
that of his two predecessors in the service of the
vernacular muse, " Ramsay and Famous Fergusson." Heroics were employed by Ramsay in
" The Gentle Shepherd," and by Fergusson in
" The Farmer's Ingle," etc. Mr. J. H. Millar
finds Burns weaker than his two Scottish fore-
runners in handling rhymed heroics ; but if Burns
did move in this measure with tread slower and
more heavy than other poets, it was because he
carried the bigger burden of thought and imagery.
Carlyle, who was severe with his poets, found Burns

at his best in the picture of " The World of Rain
and Ruin," resulting from the thaw among the
upland sources of the Ayr, which should complete
the fall of the rival bridge :—

> Then down ye'll hurl, deil nor ye never rise !
> And dash the gumlie jaups up to the pouring skies.

W. CRAIBE ANGUS—A TRUE SCOT.

11TH DECEMBER, 1899.

> DECEMBER'S cauld has chilled a heart,
>   An' taen a life sae hard to spare,
> Sae sair for us frae him to part,
>   And list his wisdom never mair.
> Oor Craibe's gane ; we kent his worth,
>   The mind and brain that overflowed ;
> Nae better man frae time cam' forth,
>   Nae better spirit gaed life's road.
>
> The changefu' years bring sorrow near
>   To ane an' a' wi' lichtnin' speed ;
> Life's cark an' care we dinna fear—
>   We sorrow ower oor Craibe, deid.
> He met the world in conflict keen,
>   He hated a' its puny ways ;
> Deceit an' sham an' a' things mean
>   He fought an' worsted a' his days.
>
> Big, breezy, bold, an' wond'rous kind,
>   Wi' piercin' eye that glowed wi' fire ;
> A giant, wi' a giant's mind,
>   Justice and truth his life's desire.
> Nane shall we ken in years to come,
>   Nane trust we as we trusted him ;
> His name we'll cherish where we roam,
>   Nor let its lustre e'er grow dim.

How can ye tell his virtues a',
　　That shone wi' glitter sure an' bricht ?
Though his loved voice is faur awa',
　　His spirit rules wi' a' his micht.
And aye in days to come we'll hear
　　The echo o' his counsel wise,
Till a' the darkness is made clear,
　　An' a' life's mystery open lies.

His wisdom was o' Nature's ain,
　　Deep rooted to the earth's fair charms ;
Nor looked he ever wi' disdain
　　On simple art from Nature's arms.
The beauty of the artist's line,
　　The simple song from human heart,
All spoke to him, with voice divine,
　　Of Nature, mother of all art.

We measure men by gear an' cash—
　　Alas ! the world nae better kens ;
We beck and bow to sorry trash,
　　And to dead heroes make amen's.
This is the world ; " the pith o' sense
　　An' pride o' worth " we canna see,
Till Death it comes and Justice len's
　　Her balance unto you and me.
　　　　　　　　　　　H. PATERSON BAYNE.

JEAN ARMOUR.

As a life partner, no one was better suited to get
along with the whims and shortcomings of the poet.
She made for him a happy home—as happy as she
could—and bore up bravely under her sorrows when
she saw the crisis of her life at hand and the cer-
tainty of widowhood faced her. She was a true

woman, a good wife, an affectionate mother; and her memory deserves to receive more of the praise so generously lavished on some of the other loves of the poet than it has yet received.

He immortalized her in many of his songs; he wove a laurel wreath around her as beautiful and enduring, if not as tragic, as that which he wove around Highland Mary. But there was one difference that speaks volumes for Jean's supremacy in his heart. While he sang of her, she was before him with all the faults, frailties, and shortcomings of humanity; all the tedium, as it has been called, of ordinary daily life, while the other had passed through the veil and so become idealized long before the "lingering star" aroused in him such a force of agonized thought, and in time impelled the world, as a result of his burning words, to elevate the Highland lass into one of the heroines of poetry. And here we might, for the sake of "Bonnie Jean," pause a moment to think how she well repaid the poet for the elevation on which his genius and his love placed her, by her rare devotion to his memory. She has been blamed because before her marriage she was imprudent; of that we cannot pretend to estimate the gravity and extent, we can only judge her by other women, by trying to imagine what another woman would have done in her place with such a suitor as Robert Burns in the very heyday of his passion-power and with his ideas of female purity shattered by his Irvine experience.

But if she fell in weakness to him who became her husband, her after-life fully atoned for it. Against her wifely character not a whisper was raised, and during her long widowhood not even the clatter of Dumfries could cast a slur or raise a hint to her detriment. She survived her husband some thirty-eight years, dying March 26, 1834. Left as she was in a most helpless condition, the people of Scotland came to her aid and soon placed her beyond all fear of want, and later made her— from her standpoint—in easy circumstances. She seemed from that time to consider that she lived to guard the fame of her husband. She refused to leave the little abode in which he had died, she kept it as a show-house to such of his admirers as visited Dumfries, and devoted herself, heart and soul, to the training of his—their children. How nobly she succeeded is well-known. Some were taken from her in early life, and laid to rest beside their father, but she was permitted to see others make their way to honourable positions in the world, while as the sunset began to fall, she found herself the almost sainted centre of her children's children. She gave of her means liberally in charity, the attentions she received from high and low never affected her native good sense, and her home was a picture of content.

PETER ROSS, LL.D.

AS ITHERS SEE HIM.

MUCH has been said, and much has been written, of Robert Burns in the last hundred years. But to one thoroughly familiar with his life, there is always something left unsaid. And of the hundreds of orations to be delivered, many will consist of a threshing over the old straw. Two-thirds of them will be delivered by ministers of the Calvinistic Orthodoxy, who seldom touch upon the real life and character of the man.

Strange that Scottish organisations should select this class of men for such a purpose, when of all men " the lads in black " were the subject of the poet's most bitter sarcasm—

> But I gae mad at their grimaces,
>   Their sighin', cantin', grace-proud faces ;
> Their three-mile prayers, an' half-mile graces—
>   Their raxin conscience,
> Whase greed, revenge and pride disgraces
>   Waur nor their nonsense.

Scotland is indebted to Robert Burns for much of her religious evolution. He practically drowned out their fire-and-brimstone hell, and ridiculed their personal devil into obscurity, until ministers were ashamed to mention either from their pulpits. The effect of this sarcasm is a more humane doctrine and a more tolerant attitude from the pulpit toward the man who refused to listen to " their nonsense."

MRS. PEROCHON.

THE piece of ground first occupied by the remains
of the Poet had been purchased by him some years
before his death for a family burial place; and when,
in 1815, his dust was re-interred below the
Mausoleum, the plot was given by Mrs. Burns to a
respected friend, Monsieur Perochon, whose wife
was daughter of the Poet's kind patroness, Mrs.
Dunlop; and Mrs. Perochon, in accordance with
her dying wish, was laid in the tomb of her mother's
friend. Mrs. Perochon's husband was a French
Royalist, who fled from his native country during
its revolutionary troubles, and found a pleasant
retreat at Castlebank, Dumfries. He was an
estimable gentleman, and, though deprived of eye-
sight, possessed of many accomplishments. Like
her mother, Mrs. Perochon was a warm-hearted,
generous, and estimable lady. After the death of
Burns the friendship between her and Mrs. Burns
was still continued, and it was specially manifested
by the former in zealous efforts to benefit the
Poet's widow and family, and which the latter
lovingly acknowledged. "Much, indeed," wrote
Mrs. Burns to Mrs. Perochon on the 2nd of February, 1816, " do I already owe to your disinterested
friendship; and while a generous public are anxious
to do justice to the genius of my husband, by building so superb a monument to perpetuate his
memory, you have paid the best tribute of your

regard by so warmly interesting yourself in behalf
of his widow and his children.   In this you follow
the example of her whose virtues you inherit, and
who highly distinguished Mr. B. by a friendship
which formed one of his first enjoyments."

JOHN ANDERSON, OF SONG FAME.

JOHN ANDERSON, the hero of one of Burns' sweetest
and most touching songs, lies buried in the churchyard of Fort Augustus, a quiet spot embosomed in
hills, and sloping down towards the wide expanse
of Loch Ness.   He was a native of Ayrshire, a
carpenter by trade, and is commonly said to have
made Burns' coffin, at the latter's own request,
many years before his death.   Anderson, to whom
Burns was warmly attached, went to Inverness-
shire after his wife's death, to reside with his
daughter Kate, who had married the innkeeper at
Invergarry, some eight miles from this village.
There he spent his declining years ; and thither
the Poet, on one of his visits to the Highlands,
came to visit his humble friend.   He rested for a
night at his house ; and local tradition still tells
how his pony wandered astray during the night,
and points out the spot, in the wildest part of the
romantic glen of Garry, where it was found and
restored to its master.   From Invergarry Burns
rode over the hills to Foyers, where he penned, or
rather pencilled (as he tells us himself) the well-

known lines with which the sight of the majestic
falls inspired his muse.

The following inscription marks the grave of
John Anderson in Fort Augustus churchyard :—

> Sacred to the Memory of John Anderson,
> Who died at Invergarry, the 4 May, 1832,
> aged 84 years :
> also his daughter Catherine, who died at Invergarry,
> the 20 December, 1832,
> aged 52 years.
> Relict of the James Grearson
> Who was lost in the " Comet " off Gourock Point
> the 21 October, 1825.
> This stone is erected by their affectionate children.

" JOHN ANDERSON, MY JO."

SOME ORIGINAL VERSES.

SOME years ago a Presbyterian minister born in
Scotland and educated in Ohio told me of a stanza
supplementary to the accepted version of " John
Anderson, my Jo," which had been composed by a
man of ordinary education whom he chanced to
meet, and who, in the estimation of those who knew
him, was regarded as just a little " off." If so,
it only goes to furnish an illustration of the well-
known adage that genius is often closely allied to

madness. It is well-known that the thought
embodied in " John Anderson, my Jo," as well as
the air, existed long before Burns recast it in the
mould of his genius, and gave it the imperishable
form in which it will endure for all time. In this
respect it resembles " Auld Lang Syne." These
songs were evoked out of simple original elements
until they reached the fullness of their maturity
under the inspiration and the genius of the Ayrshire
Bard.

The author of the subjoined stanza said that the
verse—

" John Anderson, my Jo, John,
    We've clamb the hill thegither,
And mony a canty day, John,
    We've had wi' ane anither ;
Now we maun totter down, John,
    But hand in hand we'll go,
And we'll sleep the gither at the foot,
    John Anderson, my Jo "—

impressed him with a sense of incompleteness that
it raised a presumption that something more should
have been said which had been left unsaid. He
therefore ventured to add the following :—

" John Anderson, my Jo, John,
    We winna mind that sleep,—
The grave sae still and cauld, John,—
    The spirit canna keep ;
But we will mount aboon, John,
    And young again we'll grow,
And ever live in blissfu' sweet,
    John Anderson, my Jo."

Some time ago another stanza was repeated to me of whose authorship I know nothing. It possesses some merit, and may be given with the foregoing :—

" John Anderson, my Jo, John,
    They say it's forty year
    Since you ca'ed me your love, John,
    And I ca'ed you my dear ;
    I think they're surely wrang, John,
    It's no' sae lang ago—
    It's just a wee bit honeymoon,
    John Anderson, my Jo."

Sentiment begets sentiment ; and pathos, pathos. The poetic instinct lies deep in the Scottish heart, and here and there a spark when struck may find the fuel at hand for a flame. Sometimes songs like legends grow. They become modified in order to adjust themselves to conditions representing the varying consciousness of humanity ; eliminations, substitutes, and additions result in a more perfect product, and at last a master mind like Burns' gives them a finishing touch, and leaves them a " thing of beauty and joy forever."

Prof. JAMES K. PATTERSON.

"AULD LANG SYNE" IN FRENCH.

THE French have always been enthusiastic admirers of Scottish poetry, but their attempts to translate them into their own language are not always very successful, as the following rendering of "Auld Lang Syne" will show :—

>   Doit-on negliger ses amis,
>   Outrager la tendresse,
>   De ceux qu'on cherissoit jadis,
>   Aux jours de ja la jeunesse ?

>   Aux jours de la jeunesse, ami ?
>   Aux jours de la jeunesse !
>   Qu'un doux verre encore, soit rempli
>   Aux jours de la jeunesse.

>   Nous courions sur le gazon,
>   Cueillant les fleurs sans cesse ;
>   Mais quels penibles pas fait-on
>   Depuis la jeunesse !
>   Aux jours, etc.

>   Nous voila qui roulons dans l'onde,
>   Quand l'ete nous oppresse ;
>   La mer, en nous separant, gronde
>   Depuis la jeunesse.
>   Aux jours, etc.

>   Embrassons-nous donc, cher ami !
>   Ma main la votre presse ;
>   Buvons un verre tout rempli
>   Aux jours de la jeunesse.
>   Aux jours, etc.

Re-translated, somewhat literally, the song would read thus :—

> Must one neglect one's friend,
>   Should we forget the tender feelings
> Of those whom we formerly loved,
>   In the days of our youth ?
>   In the days of our youth !
>   Let a sweet glass again be filled
>   To the days of our youth.
>
> We ran upon the grass,
>   Pulling flowers unceasingly ;
> But oh ! what tedious journeys we've had
>   Since the days of our youth.
>
> We played in the water
>   When the summer sun oppressed us.
> The sea, now separating us, has been roaring
>   Since the days of our youth.
>
> Let us embrace then, dear friend !
>   Let my hand press yours.
> Let us drink a glass quite full
>   To the days of our youth.

HIGHLAND MARY.

> I WOULD I were the light fern growing
>   Beneath my Highland Mary's tread,
> I would I were the green tree, throwing
>   Its shadow o'er her gentle head !
> I would I were a wild flower, springing
>   Where my sweet Mary loves to rest,
> That she might pluck me while she's singing,
>   And place me on her snowy breast !

I would I were in yonder heaven
  A silver star, whose soft dim light
Would rise to bless each summer even,
  And watch my Mary all the night !
I would, beneath these small white fingers,
  I were the lute her breath has fanned—
The gentle lute, whose soft note lingers,
  As loth to leave her fairy hand !

Ah, happy things ! ye may not wander
  From Scotland to some darker sky,
But ever live, unchanging, yonder,
  To happiness and Mary nigh !
While I at midnight sadly weeping
  Upon its deep transparent blue,
Can only gaze while all are sleeping,
  And dream my Mary watches too !

LADY STIRLING MAXWELL.

MARY CAMPBELL, daughter of Archibald and Annie Campbell, was born near Dunoon, on the lower Clyde, probably in 1764. She died in October, 1786. Burns and she parted May 14th, 1786. She was on her way back from the Highlands, when she took fever, and died in the house of a relative in Greenock. Her father was bitterly opposed to Burns ; and after Mary's death burned everything connected with the Poet—many letters and snatches of songs, etc. She had an only sister, Annie, twelve years old. Annie used to sing those songs thus sent. They seemed never to have been in writing after the original were burned ; and Burns was careless about his manuscripts. From the fact of

William Motherwell copying them from recitation,
in the house of one of Anderson's sons, many years
after, I judge they were not in Burns' printed
works. But they are gone. Motherwell died
soon after, and they appear to be lost. The
elegant pocket Bible, in two volumes, Burns gave
to Mary at parting, with a lock of Mary's flaxen
hair in one of them, the mother gave to two daughters of Annie's, telling them that they would get a
" chest of drawers " for them when they set up
housekeeping. Their brother, William Anderson,
got them from the sisters by a present of £5 to each
of them, and brought the Bible and the lock of
hair to Caledon township, Ontario. Getting in
distress for money, he accepted $100 for them—
raised in 1840 by some patriotic Scotsmen in
Montreal, who sent them to Scotland.

The father never relented in his hostility to
Burns, but the mother did, and used to sing the
song of " Highland Mary." She had been told
he was "wild and profane," but, remembering the
one interview she had with him, said, "but he was a
real warm-heartit chiel." Of Mary's personal
appearance her relatives testify that she was of a
good height, very high coloured, and of amiable,
retiring disposition. Her mother always dwelt
on the quality of truthful sincerity in her daughter,
and a cousin of the mother, Mrs. Macpherson, in
whose house Mary died, spoke of her as an " angel
in the house." Three years after Mary's death,

Burns penned the immortal song of " Highland Mary," and in 1792 the ode " To Mary in Heaven." Three or four other songs that Scotland " will not willingly let die " he wrote in her honour.

Rev. W. WYE SMITH.

HIGHLAND MARY'S BIBLE AT ALLOWAY.

AMONG the relics in the Monument at Alloway is the Bible, in two volumes, given by Burns to Highland Mary.   On the fly-leaf of the first volume is written, in the Poet's handwriting: " ' And ye shall not swear by my name falsely : I am the Lord.' —Levit. xix. 12." In the second volume : " ' Thou shalt not forswear thyself, but shall perform unto the Lord thine oath.'—Matt. v. 33." And in both volumes is written, " Robert Burns, Mossgiel," with his Mason-mark appended. In one of the volumes is preserved a lock of Highland Mary's hair.

These volumes came into possession of Mary's mother, and were kept in the family. William Anderson, mason, Renton, near Dumbarton, a grandson, took them with him to Canada in 1834. Circumstances forced him to part with them, after being assured they would be carefully treasured beyond the risk of loss or destruction. A party of gentlemen in Montreal bought them for £25, and sent them to the Provost of Ayr for presentation to the Monument.   On Thursday, 24th December, 1840, they were formally presented to Provost

Limond, at a dinner in honour of the occasion; and on the Poet's birthday, 25th January, 1841, were delivered to the custodier of the Monument, at a public dinner, in the Burns Arms Inn, Alloway.

SCOTLAND'S LESSON.

SOME sixty years ago Scotland thought she had found one akin to Robert Burns in Anderson, a railroad labourer, who wrote under the name of " The Surfaceman." He was taken from the railroad and made assistant librarian in the Edinburgh University. Scotland was determined not to repeat her neglect of another supposed genius. Alas ! he was like a thrush that had been captured and caged. His song ceased, and little or nothing was ever heard from " The Surfaceman " afterward.

We therefore wonder if Scotland would have been so rich as she is to-day in poetry and song had Robert Burns found a life of ease and plenty. Would he have ceased to note that —

> Man's inhumanity to man
> Makes countless thousands mourn ?

Would we have lost his spirit of independence, and regretted having written —

> The rank is but the guinea's stamp,
> The man's the gowd for a' that ;

And his bold declaration—

> For me, before a monarch's face
> Ev'n there I winna flatter ?

Would the desire still have existed—

> That I, for puir auld Scotland's sake,
> Some usefu' plan or book could make,
>   Or sing a sang at least ?

Would he still have cried out

> " O Scotia ! my dear, my native soil !
> For whom my warmest wish to heaven is sent,
> Long may thy hardy sons of rustic toil
> Be blest with health, and peace, and sweet
>   content?"

Who can tell ?   Our hearts go out in pity and sympathy for the trials and cares of Robert Burns, but we feel that Scotland and the world at large is richer at least from the sterling independence manifested throughout all his works.

Early in life he nailed his colours to the mast. We rejoice to think that he went down with the flag of liberty and independence still flying.

ROBERT   HOWDEN.

WILSON'S PRINTING PRESS.

THE printing press on which the first edition of the Poems was printed, at Kilmarnock, in 1786, by John Wilson, was taken to Ayr on his removal to start the *Ayr Advertiser*.   It has never been out of the possession of successive proprietors of the paper, and being made of solid oak, the occasion

E

of the centenary in 1859 suggested to Mr. Thomas M. Gemmell, its owner, the idea to convert it into something useful and ornamental. The result was a beautiful drawing-room chair, which was occupied at the centenary dinner, in the County Buildings, Ayr, by the chairman, Sir James Fergusson, Bart. The two arms represent *The Twa Dogs*, carved from drawings by Mr. Robertson, animal painter, Glasgow. The spiral ivy-twined pillars that run up on either side of the back are capped by miniature models of *Tam o' Shanter* and *Souter Johnny*. The under part of the back is stuffed, but higher up, in the form of a medallion, there is richly engraved, on wood, the scene at the keystone of the *Auld Brig*, when *Cutty Sark* seizes the tail of Tam's mare. A semi-circular silver scroll round the base of the medallion contains a history of John Wilson's printing press, signed by Thomas M. Gemmell, proprietor, and D. M. Lyon, foreman, *Ayr Advertiser* printing office. Surmounting all, and relieved by thistle and holly leaf carving, rises a miniature bust of Burns, after Nasmyth's portrait; underneath which a small silver shield contains these lines engraved from *The Vision* :—

> " ' *And wear thou this*,' she solemn said,
> And bound the *holly* round my head ;
> The polish'd leaves, and berries red,
>   Did rustling play ;
> And, like a passing thought, she fled
>   In light away."

NEIL GOW.

A NOTED fiddler of Burns' time, whom the Poet has celebrated both in prose and verse, was Neil Gow, whose acquaintance he made on his Northern tour.   The meeting is recorded in his journal, under date Friday, August 31, 1787 :—

"Walk with Mrs. Stewart and Beard to Birnam top—fine prospect down Tay—Craigbarns Hills— Hermitage on the Bran Water, with a picture of Ossian—breakfast with Dr. Stewart—Neil Gow plays ; a short, stout-built Highland figure, with his greyish hair shed on his honest, social brow— an interesting face, making strong sense, kind, open-heartedness,   mixed   with   unmistrusting simplicity—visit his house—Margaret Gow."

Nathaniel Gow was sixty years of age when Burns saw him, having been born at Inver, near Dunkeld, in 1727.   He died in 1807.

In the following verse Gow is alluded to as having put down the fashion for foreign music, which, towards the end of the eighteenth century, had sprung up among the fashionable and middle classes in Scotland :—

> But a royal ghaist, wha ance was cas'd
>   A prisoner aughteen year awa',
> He fir'd a fiddler in the North
>   That dang them tapsalteerie O !

The allusion in these lines is to James I. of

Scotland, a Royal poet and musician, whose spirit, our bard tells us, had entered into and animated "a fiddler in the North," thereby meaning Neil Gow, whose strathspeys and reels dang the Continental airs "tapsalteerie O!" Long may they continue to do so, and more power to them.

JOHN MUIR.

JAMES GOULD.

JAMES GOULD, the well-known Burns' collector, died at Edinburgh on the 25th of March, 1890. For 35 years (1850-85) he was assistant manager of the "Cross" Post Office. While engaged in the post office Mr. Gould began to collect interesting memoranda in connection with Burns, and in his labours in this department evinced a persistency which has been held to amount to absolute genius. With respect to his "Burnsiana," as his Burns collections are called, he has been the means of gathering together materials which, in connection with the Poet, will be consulted by all future students who desire to make their study complete regarding the bard or his poetry. Included in the collection are the genuine autographs of those who presided at the various centenary meetings in 1859, and also those of the Poet's relatives living at the time, besides many eminent men in literature, science, and art, who took part in the celebrations —in all, about three hundred. For these Mr. Gould penetrated into the obscurest corner of every British settlement, also into portions of the American States, Africa, and India. The first four of these interesting volumes have been deposited in the Mitchell Library, Glasgow, and six other volumes have only recently been completed. Besides the " Burnsiana," Mr. Gould also compiled other interesting volumes, such as the " Old Merket Cross," Edinburgh ; " The High Street Calamity, Edinburgh," 1861 ; " St. Giles' Cathedral," previous to and after restoration, 1883 ; " Stray Green Leaves," an extraordinary collection of poetical pieces printed with autograph, the latter from the authors. For years Mr Gould suffered from impaired health, being often months together in the sick chamber, but he steadily persevered with his favourite compilations until almost the hour of his death.

A HORACE GREELEY TRIBUTE.

New York, January 16th, 1870.

Dear Sir,—I have never failed to attend a Burns' Dinner when prior engagements did not prohibit, as they do this year.

Let me only say that each year extends and diffuses the fame of the Peasant Poet, who, through all the years of my life, has been Scotland's greatest glory, and I beg leave to offer this tribute to his genius :

The peasant rhymer, who first taught the proud and great to find human nature in the poor and lowly.

Yours, etc.,

HORACE GREELEY.

To Andrew H. H. Dawson, Esq.

CAPTAIN GROSE, THE ANTIQUARY.

ON May 12th, 1791, died the once famous Francis Grose, antiquary, artist, and humourist—a man whose name is even unknown, but who lives in the poetry of his friend Burns, and in the antiquarian literature of these islands. He was born, in 1731, at Greenford, Middlesex, and was the son of Francis Grose, a native of Berne, who came to England in the eighteenth century and settled at Richmond, Surrey. He received a classical education, and he studied art in Shipley's drawing school. As early as 1766 he became a member of the Incorporated Society of British Artists, and in 1768 he exhibited a drawing, "High Life Below Stairs," In the next year he exhibited architectural drawings in the Royal Academy.

About this time Grose held the office of Richmond Herald, and subsequently he was adjutant and paymaster of the Hampshire Militia. His system of keeping the regimental accounts was an original one—he put all receipts into one pocket, and made

all his payments from another—and this soon
landed him in confusion and difficulty.   He adopted
the same system when, in 1778, he was made
adjutant and captain of the First Surrey, or the
Tangier Regiment.   In his own money matters he
was equally careless, and the fortune which his
father left him soon vanished.

In 1773 appeared the first volume of the work on
which his chief fame rests—"The Antiquities
of England and Wales."   This was completed in
four volumes, in 1787, and still remains a standard
work.   The drawings were made by himself, but
he had assistance in writing the descriptions.
This work completed, he visited Scotland, where,
at Friar's Carse, he made the acquaintance of
Robert Burns, and the two soon became cronies.
Grose was immensely corpulent, "full of good
humour and good nature, and an inimitable boon
companion," and in Burns he found a kindred
spirit, who, however, did not scruple to satirize
his friend.   To Grose the Poet addressed the well-
known poem which begins—

> Hear, Land o' Cakes, and brither Scots
> Frae Maidenkirk to Johnny Groat's ;
> If there's a hole in a' your coats,
>   I rede you tent it ;
> A chiel's amang you, takin' notes,
>   And, faith, he'll prent it !

The second verse describes the captain's personal
appearance and his skill with the pencil—

> If in your bounds ye chance to light
> Upon a fine, fat, fodgel wight,
> O' stature short, but genius bright—
>   That's he ; mark weel—
> And wow ! he has an unco slight
>   O' cauk and keel.

Burns gave serious offence to the worthy antiquary by another poem, " Ken ye ought of Captain Grose ? "

In the introduction to the " Antiquities of Scotland," Grose says that Burns made out what was most worthy of notice in Ayrshire, and also wrote specially for him, in connection with Alloway Kirk, " Tam o' Shanter," one of the most popular of the Poet's works. (See Burns' General Correspondence, Letter 227.)

The " Antiquities of Scotland " (2 vols.) were published in 1789-1791. Then the author visited the sister isle ; but alas ! his work here was soon cut short. He had not written and printed more than seven pages of his " Antiquities of Ireland," when he died of apoplexy in Dublin. His remains lie in Drumcondra Church.

THE GREENOCK BURNS CLUB.

" THE Mother Club " was instituted, and held its first anniversary meeting, in 1802. Since the year 1885, when it was re-formed and re-constructed on a wider and more useful basis, the club has

never ceased to prosper in its membership, in its
finances, in its mission. It has held meetings four
times a year regularly, it has observed the Poet's
anniversary without a single omission, it has had
its delightful summer picnics, it has fostered the
study of Scottish history and poetry (especially
ballad poetry) among the rising generation by the
presentation, after competition, of valuable prizes
for knowledge and efficiency in recitation ; it has
frequently contributed sums in aid of local charities,
and it has kept alive a most desirable spirit of Scottish nationality in the community. It may be
said to be the most cosmopolitan society in the
towns of Greenock and Port-Glasgow—quite a
number of prominent gentlemen belonging to the
latter place are included in the membership. It
is cosmopolitan in this respect, that in religion it
knows no creed or sect, in politics it recognises no
particular party. Thus it is that at quarterly
meetings, and also anniversary gatherings on that
night when

> " A blast o' Janwar win'
>   Blew hansel in on Robin,"

Whigs and Tories a' agree. Conservatives who
think that politics begins and ends with them,
Liberals who imagine that they are the salt of the
earth, and Radicals who maintain that they, and
they alone, have the salvation of the country in

their hands—all these meet on a common level of Caledonianism, with the author of "Tam o' Shanter" as the "keystane" of the social arch. Snobbery is, as far as may be, at a discount at a symposium of Burns' admirers. The Poet's spirit is then in the air, and every man is as good as his neighbour. Yet this feeling of democracy—this tacit confession that a man's a man for a' that—does not interfere with the fusion of the Poet's devotees. The club has, in recent years particularly, drawn about as much support from West-end mansions as from the flats and half-flats of the shopkeepers and better class of clerks and workmen resident in every ward of the town.

The club has property, too, and a habitation, as well as a kenspeckle name. Its principal meeting room in Nicolson Street is a dream of beauty—a suggestion of the artist and the antiquary. Attractive, in some instances valuable, pictures in oil, water-colour, and photography of past hon. presidents and presidents, of prominent members of the club, of famous honorary members literally cover the walls. Among these are Professor Blackie, Lord Rosebery, Andrew Carnegie, Oliver Wendell Holmes, Lord Tennyson, Andrew Lang, Sir Noel Paton—one of whose pictures also graces the right side at the fireplace—Professor Masson, Sir Henry Irving, J. M. Barrie, Colin Rae Brown, Sir Andrew Lusk, Professor Schipper (Vienna), Professor Auguste Angellier (Lille), Rev. Dr. Hugh

Macmillan, Dr. W. C. Smith (author of " Olrig Grange "), " Ian Maclaren," Professor Saintsbury, Right Hon. A. J. Balfour, J. Logie Robertson (" Hugh Halliburton "), C. Martin Hardie, R.S.A., Rudyard Kipling, Colonel John Hay (Washingtion), Sir Donald Currie, Neil Munro, Dr. Robertson Nicoll (of the " British Weekly "), Hon. J. H. Choate, Dr. John D. Ross, Sir Henry Craik, Colonel Scott, C.B., Sir James Sivewright, General Sir Archibald Hunter, Sir Thos. Lipton, Dr. Robert Caird, Sir George Reid, R.S.A., Sir Thomas Sutherland, Mr. Durward Lely, etc. The collection includes a number of canvasses, chiefly in oil, of Scottish scenes, also a few local pictures, old spinning wheels, curling stones, besides other articles of interest relating to the time in which Burns lived. An old oaken brass-bound chest, placed near the well-stocked bookcase, contains the club's manuscripts, minute-books, and other papers and relics. The principal treasure, perhaps, in this chest is the original minute-book of the Greenock Club, the first entries in which are dated 1801, in the summer of which year the society was first formed. It is an Excise book, which belonged to Robert Burns, or rather was in his keeping and for his use as a Government servant. It is of the once familiar form, oblong and narrow in width, and bound in thick brown calf boards. The leaves have taken on an age-worn appearance, but otherwise the little volume is in a state of good preservation. On the first leaf, under the top cover, is the following inscription :—" This book was found in the house of the late Mr. Robert Burns at his demise, and presented to the Burns Club of Greenock by Adam Pearson, Esq., of His Majesty's Excise, Edinburgh, A.D. 1801." On the second page is the following, in large and legible handwriting : " Greenock Burns Club and Ayrshire Society." The minutes in this book open with an ode on the Poet composed by Mr. Neil Dougal, a prominent and gifted local musician of the early years of the last century, and the author of some psalm tunes long popular with Presbyterians, including the well-known " Kilmarnock." The long ode—oh, how lengthy and gushing these old odes on Burns usually were !—concludes as follows :

> " Sae for his [Burns] sake, the dainty cheil,
> I wish his weans and widow weal,
> Gude grant them wealth
>   O' milk and meal
>   For brose and bread,
> And bless them with a cosy beil
>   Till they are dead."

Homely, yet quite expressive, and a trifle quaint ! This entry is signed by " Robert Barr," who appears to have acted as the first of the long list of secretaries. The next item in the minute-book, " Presented by Mr. Pearson, of Edinburgh," gives a

brief account of the first " anniversary celebration,"
as it is called even in those early days. It says :
" On Friday, 29th January, 1802, the club held
their anniversary celebration of the birth of the
Bard "—Greenock men were apparently at that
time ignorant of the fact that Burns was born on
the 25th of that month. The minute-writer goes
on to say that about forty members sat down to
a " sumptuous repast " in the White Hart Hotel,
under the presidency of Mr. John Wright, who
proposed the toast of the Poet, and recited an ode—
the usual long-drawn-out, winding, word-spun
ode. The book shows, as one turns over its stained
and yellow pages, that anniversaries were held in
1803, 1804, 1805, and 1806, and there were also
enthusiastic meetings, invariably in July and at
Hallowe'en. It ought to be mentioned that in
1804 the anniversary of the birth was also held at
Alloway, in the house in which the Poet first saw
the light, Greenock Club being present by deputa-
tion. Many entries in the book are most interesting
reading. For example, at the January celebration
of 1803 there is a presentation of books to the
society, along with copy of " the new edition " of
Burns' works, from Mr. Archibald Campbell,
brother to " Highland Mary ; " in August, 1804,
the death of Admiral Duncan, of Camperdown
fame, is intimated and entered in the book. At this
meeting " Mr. Wright stated that he had known
Robert Burns intimately for three years, and having

been associated with him in his profession he could from his personal knowledge deny most emphatically that Robert Burns was a man of intemperate or dissolute habits." In 1806 the anniversary dinner was held for the first time on 25th January, the meeting taking place in the "White Hart Inns," as the wording is. This was a remarkable gathering, for much business was transacted at it, and the minute is long and detailed. One entry has more than usual interest. It says that the club passed a message of sympathy with one of its members, Mr. Greer, and family, on "the loss of their gallant son and brother, who fell most nobly fighting for his King and country at the glorious Battle of Trafalgar." The member who proposed the motion of consolation said that "it seemed a very remarkable coincidence that while the son of one of their most esteemed members had died fighting gloriously "—Britishers were in those dangerous and stirring days jingoes unabashed and unashamed—" under Lord Nelson, the son of another member of the club had, while spared to return to his home and friends, assisted to carry the immortal and gallant Admiral from the deck mortally wounded." Details on this and a mass of other ancient and engrossing matters are in this wonderful Excise-book.

BURNS' TODDY KETTLE.

THE following correspondence is self-explanatory :

January 9, 1923.

" John M'Burnie, Esq.,

"" Secretary Dumfries Burns Club,

"" Dumfries, Scotland.

" My Dear Mr. M'Burnie and Fellow Members of the Dumfries Burns Club :

" When thinking of the birthday of the ' World's Poet ' a short time ago, it occurred to me that I would like to return to Dumfries a valuable article that belonged to our beloved Bard. Naturally, my thoughts travelled to the Dumfries Burns Club, with the result that the following telegrams were exchanged :

" ' January 3, 1923.'

" ' Desirous present Club Burns' copper kettle from his home, afterward in Globe Tavern, then Albany and Boston, and purchased by me in 1915. Highly prized Burns' relic. Will Club accept ? If so, will forward in time Burns' dinner.

" ' Walter Scott.'

" ' January 4, 1923.'

" ' Club will gratefully accept kettle, and is deeply indebted for this further generous gift from you. Send as full history as possible.

" ' M'Burnie.'

" The story of this article was told in our public press throughout the country in the year 1915,

when an estate was to be disposed of here in New
York. Friends furnished me with newspaper
clippings regarding the sale, which I attended,
purchasing the kettle. It has been viewed by
thousands since it came into my possession, not
to speak of the many more who previously had the
opportunity. The history is engraved on the
outside, and since the acceptance of the relic by
the Dumfries Burns Club I have added the closing
line. The freshly engraved portion is, of course,
much brighter than the preceding lines, but it
will become as dark as the rest of the engraving
in a short time. It is as follows :—

" ' ROBERT BURNS' TODDY KETTLE.

" ' Most prized of the Burns Relics. Copper
kettle used by Burns at his home in Dumfries.
After his death it became the property of the
Globe Tavern. Sold to John Allan of New York ;
then owned by J. V. L. Pruyn of Albany, who
presented it to his daughter. At sale of her effects
(about 1875), it was purchased by Mr. George P.
Philes, who held and treasured it until his death.
Bought at Public Sale of the Philes Collection in
February, 1915,

" ' By Walter Scott of New York,
Past Royal Chief of the Order of Scottish Clans,
and presented by him to Dumfries Burns Club,
January 25, 1923.'

" I am very happy in the thought that this

kettle will henceforth be the property of the
Dumfries Burns Club.   In a way I am sorry to
part with it, because it has occupied a conspicuous
place in my office ever since its purchase, always
creating an atmosphere of tenderness in the hearts
of those who have seen it, and serving as a constant
reminder to me of the author of the 'World's
Doxology.'   However, I believe it should go back
to Dumfries—the last earthly home of our beloved
Poet—and find a final resting-place among other
articles used by him.

—WALTER SCOTT."

BURNS' POVERTY.

WAS IT REAL OR IMAGINARY ?

THE belief that throughout the whole of his career
Burns was a very poor man, who in the end died
practically a pauper, is so universally received as an
incontrovertible fact that to seek to dispute it
is looked upon, even in Burns circles, as the rankest
of heresies.   Why this should be so is not very
evident, for whatever additional lustre may be
thought to be thrown upon Burns' achievements
by the untowardness of his environment is more
than counterbalanced by the vague imaginings
of what he might have accomplished in more
favouring circumstances, as well as by the Southern's sneers at the neglect he experienced at the
hands of the literary patrons of his day.   Burns'

poverty is, however, more imaginary than real
when brought to the test of proof, more especially
in the closing decade of his life. He cleared £500
by the Edinburgh edition, which was no incon-
siderable sum to a man in his position when we
allow for differences in value then and now. Of
this sum he lent £200 to his brother Gilbert, of
which more anon. When he became an exciseman
his ostensible salary was about 50 pounds a year,
but this leaves out of calculation certain other
emoluments arising from prosecutions and seizures,
which, on the average, yielded more than the
official salary of an exciseman of that period.
Robert Chambers sets down Burns' average income
in Dumfries at £80, but Mr. Macfadyan, of the
Scottish Inland Revenue, who has carefully investi-
gated the matter, is inclined to think that, year
with year, it was more than double that figure.
Certain it is that he lived in Dumfries with considerable pretensions to gentility. He latterly
rented a self-contained house, and, good reports
and bad reports allowed for, he moved in good
society. True, we read of him now and again
requesting small pecuniary loans from his personal
friends, but that need not surprise anyone con-
versant with the Poet's characteristic open-handed-
ness wherever money was concerned. " Coin his
pouches widna bide in ; " whenever he was in
funds there were corresponding wants to supply,
as witness his orders for books to Peter Hill, and

certain other of his letters bearing on personal expenditure. His extreme nervousness about the seven pounds odds owing to Williamson, the draper, legal notice of which he received a few days before his death, must be credited to the physical conditions under which he laboured, and it is the hysterical tone of the letters he then wrote in apprehension of extreme proceedings being taken against him that has given colour to the time-worn tradition that he died literally without a penny in his possession. The truth is that he had no sufficient reason to fear " the horrors of a jail," the fact of the draper's account having found its way into the hands of a lawyer being satisfactorily explained by a dissolution of partnership, of which previous notice had been given. Burns' exact financial position on his deathbed is fortunately preserved in a series of documents, mostly in the autograph of his brother Gilbert, which recently came under the notice of the writer, and which do not appear to have seen the light before, though they were on exhibition in Dumfries in 1880, when funds were being raised for the local statue of the Poet. The documents are eleven in number, the most interesting being a statement of the financial position of Gilbert as at the date of his brother's death, when the trust estate was formed for behoof of Jean and her children ;   another showing the accounting between Gilbert and the Poet between 1792 and 1797, the balance owing being acknowledged over Jean's signature; and, third, a corrected copy of the foregoing, brought down to May, 1798, also signed by Jean, and containing a declaration signed by Gilbert and William Thomson, writer, on behalf of the trustees. Gilbert's debt was not discharged till 1820; another of the documents, in the form of a letter from Gilbert to Jean, bringing out the balance owing as at 16th December, 1820, at £220 7s 6d. It has hitherto been the general impression that Gilbert repaid his loan of £200 by a single payment on receipt of his editorial fee for the edition of Currie which bears his name; but that is not the fact. If, as has been often stated, the loan was granted in 1788, it is certain that the bill was drawn out on 21st December, 1792, from which date down to the death of the Poet Gilbert credits himself with "per contra" sums, in apparent accordance with a verbal agreement come to between them. Some of these entries are exceedingly interesting. For instance, we learn that the Poet paid regularly for the "bed, board, washing, clothes, books, and school wages" of "dear bought Bess," who was brought up by his mother and Gilbert. He also seems to have settled an annuity upon his mother, the sum of £5 being charged against him under that head down to the very day of his death. The exact balance owing by Gilbert when the Poet died is set down at £183 16s. 7d.; immediately following the death, however, sundry payments on behalf of the family, including an advance of 10 guineas to the widow, reduces the balance to £158 15s. 5d., as at September 1, 1796. A man dying in 1796 with an assured asset of £184 (again contrasting values) could scarcely be considered as in the lowest depths of poverty unless overwhelmed on the other hand with debt. To Gilbert's statement of accounts is luckily appended a list of all the debts owing by his deceased brother as at September 1, 1796, and which were paid by him, doubtless after public advertisement in some form or other. In this list does not appear the draper's bill which had caused the Poet so much concern, and which probably had been discharged in the interim. The total amount of the Poet's debts is £14 15s., including the butcher and other tradesmen, thus leaving a free balance of £170 for the widow and children. Among these accounts appears one in name of a " Dr. Brown," amounting to £2 3s. . . . . From other entries we learn that the grave of Burns cost 2s. 6d., the mortcloth 3s., and that the sum of 5s. was paid for the tolling of the town bells. Gilbert was continually reducing his debt by payments in kind, and these became more frequent when he removed to Dinning, the family of the Poet being supplied with cheese, barley, etc., down to 1809 ; for though Gilbert went to Grant's Braes in 1801, his brother-in-law, John Begg, was left in charge of the farm down to the former date.

When the debt was finally discharged in 1820, Jean was in such comfortable circumstances that, at her request, the £200 odds was paid to the eldest son, Robert, who had involved himself in pecuniary embarrassments in London, and whose appointment in the Stamp Office was thereby placed in jeopardy.

It is also an article of current belief that Gilbert, being the more prudent of the two brothers, was the more successful from a worldly point of view. Whatever may be embraced in this assertion, it is certain that he was hard pressed for money all his life, and, all things considered, there need be no hesitation in saying that the Poet's worldly circumstances, after the dissolution of partnership at Mossgiel, were always infinitely superior to Gilbert's.

THE NASMYTH PORTRAIT.

THE Original Portrait of Robert Burns, painted by Alexander Nasmyth, while the Poet visited Edinburgh in 1787, was bequeathed to the nation by his last surviving son, Colonel William Nicol Burns, and is now in the National Gallery, Edinburgh. On the back of it is Nasmyth's own inscription :—" Painted from Mr. Robert Burns, by his friend, Alexander Nasmyth, Edinbro', April, 1787." On the same canvas is a certificate written by the Poet's eldest son :—" I hereby certify that this is the original portrait of the Poet by Alexander Nasmyth, landscape painter in Edinburgh, and is the only authentic portrait of him in existence, or at least the only portrait of the Poet whose authenticity is indisputable. Dumfries, April 8th, 1834. (Signed) ROBERT BURNS."

There are three portraits of this size painted by Nasmyth, this being the original from which all the others are copied. One was executed for George Thomson, and is now in the National Portrait Gallery, London, in the catalogue of which it is stated to have been touched upon by Sir Henry Raeburn, which does not add to its value as a portrait. The other belongs to Mr. Elias Cathcart of Auchindrane, near Ayr, and was painted in 1824, by Mr. Cathcart's permission. In addition to these, Nasmyth also painted a small Cabinet Picture—a full length portrait, as he appeared in Edinburgh at the time he sat for the original from which the likeness is taken. This painting is in the collection of Sir Hugh Hume Campbell, Bart., and is now at Marchmont. An engraving of it was taken for a vignette to Lockhart's *Life of Burns*, in *Constable's Miscellany*. The original picture has been frequently engraved,—the first time by John Beugo, for the Edinburgh edition of the poems, to whom the Poet gave sittings to improve the likeness— as the painting was then only finished to a certain extent—to obtain an engraving ; it has also been engraved by E. Mitchell and William Walker, the latter being a very beautiful specimen of mezzo-tinto engraving of a high character. Of the Original Nasmyth Portrait there is another version by Skirving, the history of which is curious. It seems that, when a boy, Skirving had seen the Poet, who was a friend of his father's ; but the Nasmyth Portrait not quite realising his recollections of Burns, he made an outline from the picture, and, taking it home, filled it up to his own idea of the expression. The result was one of Skirving's best crayon drawings, which has been engraved by Henry Robinson.

DEATH AND DR. HORNBOOK.

IT is now more than a century since Burns wrote this poem. There would, perhaps, be some difficulty in fixing the date of the poem from internal evidence, for we know that some of the productions of our Bard are sadly misleading in this respect ; but his brother states that though the Kilmarnock Edition (1786) does not contain the piece, it was written in 1785.

It may be interesting to have a look at Burns' surroundings at this period, and it is fortunate that he has given us an account of his private life at this time. Burns' father died at Lochlea in 1784, and his family, with its mother, trying to escape with something from the wreck caused by a

lawsuit, removed to Mossgiel. Here Burns lived
probably the best and the worst of his life in fifteen
months. Here he became the father of Bess, and
from this place he sallied forth to meet Jean Armour.
His first poem, which made much of a hit at the
time, the " Address to the Unco Guid," was composed over the sectarian brawls which often
disturbed the surface peace of most of the church-
yards in the West of Scotland between the sermons.
The fight must have been hot in Mauchline. It is
noteworthy that the United Presbyterians had
their beginning in the village about this time.
We may look at this period as the foundation of
Burns' poetical standing. Broadly and strongly
did he lay his base on the hearts and feelings of
the descendants of the Covenanters ; and, for a
superstructure, he sang their home life, their
church feast, their harvest home, their loves, their
cares, their crosses, their superstitions, their
everything which was dear to them. " The
Inventory " and the " Epistle to Davie " give us,
in Burns' own words, an account of his everyday
life. One qualification must be observed when
the " Epistle " is under consideration, and that
with regard to Burns' drinking. Burns was
probably writing to a " wet hand "—the thing
is more than probable—and of course he would
make his own potations look as big as possible.
The universal testimony of his friends was that
they never saw Burns drunk ; and " Poosy Nancy "

herself was greatly surprised when she heard that Burns spoke of discussing politics and whisky in her house. With regard to him " setting his staff wi' a' his skill to keep him siccar," when coming down Hood's Hill, I should like to do the same thing under the circumstances ; and, though a total abstainer, I must confess to " to leeward whiles takin' a bicker against my will," too, even in broad daylight, when walking through this classic district. The fact is, that the road is so steep, that it is very inconvenient to come down in a straight line. The old road goes over the top of the hill, but the new road, winding round the base of it, has been laid there since Burns' day. It would appear that most of the editors of Burns have been led by this change to suppose that Burns says that he was so drunk that he could hardly keep his feet on a level road. We may look on Burns as being at this time, at least, no worse than his neighbours, but not enough of a boor to deny himself the pleasure of a social night with his fellow-masons in Tarbolton.

It was on a night early in spring when Burns attended one of the meetings of the lodge, and his rival wit, John Wilson, parochial schoolmaster, etc., was also present. The two had many passes of wit, we may presume, and, as the ale loosened their tongues, the mirth grew brisker. But we are told " nae man can tether time nor tide." Twelve o'clock drew near (Forbes M'Kenzie was

not yet), and the company broke up. Burns'
road home lay over Hood's Hill. The hill was
climbed and descended in safety, save for the
bickerings noted in the text; and now the Poet
was in the very centre of a rustic scene of great
beauty. Behind him, dimly seen by the light of
the lately risen moon, lay the village of Tarbolton,
sleeping, as it still does, unless when a stranger
passes through, and then—well, let that alone.
On the right were the finely-wooded lands surround-
ing Montgomerie Castle; to the left was the mere
known as Tarbolton Loch, and right in front was
the Fail Burn, which drains the loch. The burn is
now crossed by a bridge, but probably there were
both a ford and a gangway at that date, and it
might not be quite safe for a man with a few glasses
of beer to attempt to walk this plank. Having
got to within a few yards of the burn without
having made up his mind on this question, viz.,
the fording or bridging of the stream, he sat down
on a stone to come to a final decision on the matter.
A bright thought came into his head. Wilson
had lately added the profession of medicine to his
somewhat miscellaneous labours, would it not be
possible to have a laugh at him on that score?
There, on the stone by the wayside, he composed
what is essentially a satire, which for sly humour,
broad wit, and human sympathy, is not surpassed
by anything in the language. Death met the Poet,
and told him of the new opponent he (Death)

had found in the neighbouring dominie. Death
appears in this piece, not as a " gruesome carle,"
but as one who likes to find leisure from a busy
calling to have a talk with some one who can listen.
It is remarkable, that Death does not complain
so much of lives being saved, as of ones which have
been let out by other means than his own. He
brings in some three characters whom Jock Horn-
book has despatched. The henpecked weaver's
wife is disposed of in such a way as to lead us to
suppose that her absence will be no great loss.
The laird only makes room for another. It is
when he comes to speak of the unfortunate country
girl that we see the feeling side in all its brightness :

> " She trusts hersel' to hide the shame
> In Hornbook's care ;
> Horn sends her aff tae her lang hame
> To hide it there."

Death begins to be more of a good fellow than ever
when the village clock strikes one, and the spectre
and the ploughman part.

To all appearance Burns never intended to
publish this poem. If it was his intention to
let it appear in print, its non-appearance in the
Kilmarnock Edition is scarcely comprehensible.
The likelihood is that he repeated the poem at
the next meeting of the craft ; and that the schoolmaster, then as now, was thought far too good a
mark to miss when he was shown so clearly. It

brought swift disaster to Wilson.   He had to leave
the village, and removed to Glasgow, where he
was appointed Session Clerk of the Gorbals Parish
—a better berth, no doubt, than that of schoolmaster to the heritors of Tarbolton.   His appointment shows us that Wilson must have been a man
of some ability.   Burns had probably found in
him a foeman worthy of his steel, and it is to be
regretted that he was the means of causing him to
become, for a time, a wanderer.   As has already
been said, Burns may be entirely freed from the
charge of malice on this occasion.   If his object
in publishing the poem was only a mercenary one,
why did it not appear in the first edition ?   It is
probable that the work was circulating from mouth
to mouth, and that each one who knew some of
it took it on him to parody it : and these parodies
would neither help the dominie nor the Poet :
and that Burns, in justice to himself, published the
poem, knowing that it had already done all the
mischief of which it was capable.

THE DE'IL'S AWA' WI' THE EXCISEMAN.

THE original is written on a piece of Excise paper.
The verses are said to have been composed extem-
pore by Burns at a meeting of his brother Excise-
men at Dumfries.   Lockhart, however, says it
was composed on the shores of the Solway, while
engaged watching a smuggling brig which had

put in there ; Lewars was despatched to Dumfries for a party of troopers, and another officer proceeded on a similar errand to Ecclefechan, leaving the Poet with a few men under his orders to watch the brig. "Burns," says Lockhart, "manifested considerable impatience while thus occupied, being left for many hours in a wet salt marsh, with a force which he knew to be inadequate for the purpose it was meant to fulfil. One of his friends hearing him abuse his friend Lewars, in particular, for being slow about his journey, the man answered that he also wished the devil had him for his pains, and that Burns in the meantime would do well to indite a song upon the sluggard. Burns said nothing, but after taking a few strides by himself among the reeds and shingle, rejoined the party and chanted to them the well-known ditty."

PATRICK MILLER.

A Neglected Friend of Burns.

I use the word neglected in a general sense, but in a censorious spirit I do impeach the members of our Edinburgh Burns Clubs among the " neglectfuls," in so far as this friend is never mentioned at the January festivals.

When we take a walk 'mang the crumblin' tombs of Auld Greyfriars we come to a headstone over the entrance to a grave directly facing the grave of Allan Ramsay, which bears the simple inscription :—" Patrick Miller, Esq., of Dalswinton —a man of versatile genius and ability," and, it may be added, a friend in need and deed to our Bard.

In December, 1785, Burns writes—" An unknown hand left ten guineas for the Ayrshire Bard with Mr. Sibbald, which I got. I have since discovered my generous unknown friend to be Patrick Miller, Esq., of Dalswinton." It was from this gentleman Burns farmed Ellisland, and Lockhart remarks :— " When Burns determined to give up his lease of Ellisland the kindness of the landlord rendered such a step easy of arrangement." It is interesting to note that Mr. Miller's steward at Dalswinton was the father of Allan Cunningham, with whom Burns was very friendly. Several of Burns' letters to Miller are printed in Chambers's " Burns," and two of Miller's five children are mentioned by our Poet—namely, Patrick, at whose instance Perry offered to place Burns on the list of contributors to the *Morning Chronicle ;* also William, captain in the Horse Guards, M.P. for Dumfriesshire, 1790, alluded to as " The Sodger Youth " in the election ballad, " The Five Carlines."

It was this same Mr. Miller who furnished Alexander Nasmyth, the father of Scottish landscape, and painter of the Poet, with £500 to enable him to visit Italy.

Directly opposite Ellisland is seen Dalswinton House, the seat, in his day, of Patrick Miller, and on the crest of the hill we see a monument which is known locally as " Miller's Maggot," raised to his memory. On Dalswinton Loch Miller made trial trips with one of his many inventions—the first paddle-steamer in the world. On its first voyage, according to Nasmyth, those on board were Patrick Miller, William Symington, Sir William Monteith, Robert Burns, William Taylor, and Alexander Nasmyth, while a looker-on was Henry Brougham, afterwards Lord Brougham.

Mr. Miller was in business in Edinburgh as a merchant in 1760. In 1767 he was elected a director of the Bank of Scotland, and in 1790 he became Deputy-Governor, and succeeded, by organising a new system of exchanges in London, in placing that institution on the stable basis on which it now rests. He contrived the first drill plough ever used in Britain; also a threshing machine propelled by horse-power, and an iron plough. He likewise introduced the feeding of cattle on steamed potatoes. But the thing on which he most prided himself in agriculture was the cultivation and introduction of fiorin grass hay into Scotland.

Mr. Miller was then 80 years of age, and was presented by the Agricultural Societies of Scotland with two silver vases.

He was one of the largest shareholders in the Carron Iron Company, and he is stated to have been the inventor of the carronade. In 1787 he had

built for him a vessel with five masts, fitted up
with paddle-wheels, and moved by manual labour,
This, armed with carronades, he offered to the
Government of the day, but, on their declining
the offer, he presented it to Gustavas III., King of
Sweden, who acknowledged it in an autograph
letter enclosed in a magnificent gold box, which
also contained a small packet of turnip seed,
whence sprang the first Swedish turnips ever
grown in this country. Among many honours
conferred on him was the Freedom of the Corpor-
ation by Leith Trinity House, and he is said to
have spent nearly all his fortune—put at £30,000—
on the various inventions and improvements in
which he was so actively engaged.

Such was Patrick Miller of Dalswinton, the
friend and landlord of our Rabbie. Let us keep
his grave as well as his memory green.

—JOHN T. MURDOCH.

JAMES M'KIE.

JAMES M'KIE, the well-known Burns collector
and publisher, died at his residence in Kilmarnock
on the 26th of September, 1891. He had nearly
completed his 75th year, having been born in 1816.
Few Scotsmen living or dead, if we except prominent men of genius, were so widely known as James
M'Kie, whose reverence for Burns and everything
associated with him was not unlike that which

James Boswell bestowed on Dr. Johnson, and who
in a way was almost as useful in getting the world
at large to recognise the true character of his hero.
Mr. M'Kie did not say or write much in a formal
manner, but his life-work was accomplished
equally well by the double process of collecting
and publishing. His re-production of original
editions of Burns' works did much years ago to
produce that intimate knowledge of them which is,
or rather was, possessed by the common people
of Scotland, and which foreigners have been wont
to comment on as proof alike of Burns' genius and
the capacity of his countrymen and women to
appreciate true poetry. As a collector Mr. M'Kie
knew no equal, and he either got possession of, or
could tell the exact whereabouts of, every original
edition, manuscript, or other important relic of
the Poet. The erection of the Burns monument at
Kilmarnock, with its large and interesting collection
of Burnsiana, was greatly the result of his labours,
and, in addition, he was identified with the prepara-
tion of a Burns' biography, a Burns' calendar, and
other similar works. Mr. M'Kie, who was brought
up as a bookbinder, started business for himself
first of all in Saltcoats, and there began the publication of Burns' literature, which he subsequently
carried on in Kilmarnock. He was a man of
remarkable energy, unfailing integrity and genial
manner, in whose company it was no ordinary
pleasure to be privileged to spend a social hour,

and who had a singular power of inspiring all with whom he came in contact with some of his own enthusiasm.

SOUTER JOHNNY.

In transmitting the "Tale of Tam o' Shanter" to Captain Grose, Burns quoted three witch-stories, one of which he made his basis for the "Tale!" Previous to the poem being sent to Grose, Burns was asked who "Tam" was, and replied, "who could it be but the guidman o' Shanter" (Hogg's edition of Burns, volume I., page 204). The Poet spent some of his youth at Kirkoswald when Douglas Graham and John Davidson were among the worthies of that village. Janet Kennedy, who attended the school at Kirkoswald with Burns, made the following statement after his death :—" I well recollect seeing Burns seated on the end of a bench, and seeming amused with Shanter's (all farmers then went by the name of their farms) neighbours joking him about the Alloway witches giving Johnny Davidson and him a fright on their way home from the Ayr New'rday Fair, where he had sold a horse, and put the price of it in his broad blue bonnet, which was blown off his head on going up Brown Carrick Hill amongst the gorse. It was, he thought, a risk to meet his wife after such a mishap, as she was well known, though a good woman, to have a scathing tongue, when she thought to exercise it either on her husband or faulty neighbours; but at the same time very superstitious, a firm believer in witch-craft. Her husband had to meet the emergency when he came home by telling her what a narrow escape he and John Davidson had made in their ride from the chase of the witches from Alloway Kirk, that she might be thankful to see him in life. Next morning his servant man was sent on his grey mare to seek, as directed, the lost bonnet, in which he was successful, with all the money in it. This story was well known among the neighbours at that time, long before Burns painted it in poetry."

Robert Chambers, in his excellent edition of Burns, (volume III., page 161) accepts the Graham and Davidson story. In the preface to a second edition he says: "I feel it to be ample reward for many anxious efforts to carry historic accuracy into the minutest details of the Poet's life that no error of any importance has been reported to me, neither has any remarkable omission been supplied. I have now the satisfaction of thinking that the work is as near to perfect correctness in matter of fact as the nature of the subject will permit it to be."

The finest collection of " Burnsiana " in existence (books, manuscripts, etc.) is that in the Poet's Monument at Kilmarnock, the largest part of which was purchased from Mr. James M'Kie of that town.

In this collection the writer noticed a pair of child's shoes, labelled "Made by John Davidson (Souter Johnny)." This is referred to in the catalogue of that museum, and also in the Bibliography of Burns, Kilmarnock, 1881.

W. Scott Douglas, in his elaborate and handsome edition of Burns (volume II., page 322), speaking of a visit to Kirkoswald, says, " Our attention was directed also to a tablet over the grave of ' John Davidson, shoemaker,' but we disregarded it, being certain, on the authority of Burns himself, that ' Souter Johnny ' was a resident in the town of Ayr. We were twitted with the query—' How then could Tam and the Souter get fou for weeks thegither ? ' Alas! we replied, thereby hangs a very tragic portion of the tale."

WILLIE BREW'D A PECK O' MAUT.

" IF bacchanalian songs are to be written at all," says Principal Shairp, " this certainly must be pronounced ' The king amang them a'.' But while no one can withhold admiration from the genius and inimitable humour of the song, still we read it with very mingled feelings, when we remember that perhaps it may have helped some topers since Burns' day a little faster on the road to ruin. As for the three boon companions themselves, just ten years after that night, Currie wrote, ' These three honest fellows—all men of uncommon talents

H

—are now all under the turf.' And in 1821 John Struthers, a Scottish poet little known, but of great worth and some genius, thus recurs to Currie's words :—

' Nae mair in learning Willie toils, nor Allan wakes the
       melting lay,
   Nor Rab, wi' fancy-witching wiles, beguiles the hour o'
       dawning day :
   For tho' they were na very fou, that wicked wee drap in
       the e'e
   Has done its turn ; untimely, now the green grass waves
       o'er a' the three.' "

DR. CURRIE'S EDITION OF BURNS.

THE first collected Edition of the Poetical Works and Letters of Burns, edited by James Currie, M.D., with an Account of his Life, etc., 4 volumes, 8vo., price Thirty-one Shillings and Sixpence, was published on the 12th April, 1800, for the benefit of the Poet's widow and family, and realised £1400. It has always been a favourite edition— within four years it had reached the Fourth Edition of 2000 copies each, and when the copyright expired in 1815 had passed through an Eighth Edition.

DR. CURRIE IN VIRGINIA.

IT may interest readers to know that Dr. Currie was for a time resident in Virginia. Like many another Scotsman he was a son of the manse.   He was born on May 31st, 1756, in the parish of Kirkpatrick-Fleming, Dumfriesshire, where his father was parish minister.   While a mere laddie he had visited Glasgow, and took a fancy for the strenuous business life, with which he came into contact there for the first time.   He was, therefore, induced to enter the service of a mercantile house in Virginia, but, unfortunately, the revolution began soon after, and all business became completely disorganised.   Owing to this, and also to the fact that he took the side of the loyalists, young Currie found it advisable to return to the Old World after some five years' residence in the New.   He was still only about twenty years of age, and he fell back upon an earlier plan of life by commencing the study of medicine.   He took his degree in the University of Glasgow, and settled down to practice in Liverpool.   There he soon acquired an eminent position in his profession, and his contributions to medical literature brought him fame by their literary as well as by their scientific merits.   Among his intimate friends in Liverpool he ranked Roscoe, the famous Italian scholar, author of the " Lives of Lorenzo the Magnificent, and of his son, Pope Leo X."

In 1792 Dr. Currie paid a visit to his native county of Dumfries, where he made the acquaintance of Burns, and he returned to Liverpool with an enthusiastic admiration of his new friend.   On

the death of the Poet, when he learned the condition
in which the widow and family were left, he yielded
to the urgent entreaty of many who thought him
peculiarly fitted for the task ; and, for the benefit
of the impoverished family, he brought out the
work described above. He has thus at once made
a valuable contribution to literature and established a claim upon the gratitude of all admirers of
Burns. The work must have exceeded all ex-
pectations by its popularity. The first edition,
as we have seen, appears to have been sold out
at once ; and within thirteen years a seventh
edition had been reached. It was in the midst
of this popularity that Dr. Currie died, on
August 31st, 1805.

THE CROCHALLAN FENCIBLES.

A SHORT time before Burns' introduction to
Edinburgh society, William Smellie, Lord Newton,
Charles Hay, and a few more wits of the Parlia-
ment House had founded a convivial club called
" The Crochallan Fencibles " (a mock allusion to
the Bonaparte Volunteer movement), which met
in a tavern kept by a genial old Highlandman
named " Daunie Douglas," whose favourite song
" Cro Chalien " suggested the dual designation
of the Club. Smellie introduced Burns as a member
in January, 1787. Cleghorn also appears to have
been on the muster-roll of this rollicking regiment,

which supplies a key to much of Burns' correspondence with him. How the revelry of the boon companions was stimulated and diversified may be as easily imagined as described.

—D. M'NAUGHT.

THE CAST OF THE POET'S SKULL.

SHORTLY after commencing work on the statue at Albany, New York, the sculptor received great assistance in the correct modelling of the head by the loan of a cast of the skull of the great Scottish Poet. Nearly all the other heads of Burns which have been sculptured, represent him as having a high forehead ; but the skull shows that the Poet's head was broad and massive rather than high, and in carrying out the outline of the skull correctly lies one of the charms of Mr. Caverley's design in reproducing the man as he was, and not merely an idealised figure of what he might have been.

The history of this cast of the skull of Burns is curious, and as, in connection with the unveiling of the statue, all details regarding it are of interest to our citizens, a brief narrative of the story may be acceptable.

Robert Burns died July 21st, 1796, and his remains were interred in a humble grave in St. Michael's Churchyard, Dumfries, four days later. The widow, the " Bonnie Jean " of so many of his

fine songs, erected a small headstone over the
grave. The remains rested there until 1815, when
a stately mausoleum was erected in another part
of the same churchyard to receive them. The
cost of this tomb, the most gorgeous which was ever
erected to contain the body of a poor ploughman
or farmer, was defrayed by a national subscription,
to which rich and poor heartily subscribed. When
everything was in readiness for the reception of the
body, a small party of the subscribers to the mausoleum, assisted by a few workmen, transferred the
remains of the Poet from the grave to the tomb.
The task was performed on the night of September
19th, 1815. In the same grave with the Bard lay
the bodies of two of his sons who had died in
infancy. The coffins of the boys were found nearly
entire, and were placed in shells and carried to
the mausoleum without difficulty. The coffin of
the Poet was almost completely wasted, but when
the cover was removed the body seemed perfect,
as though death had been of recent occurrence.
"The scene," it is said, "was so imposing that
most of the workmen stood bare and uncovered,
and at the same time felt their frames thrilling
with some indefinable emotion as they gazed on
the ashes of him whose fame is as wide as the world
itself. But the effect was momentary, for when
they proceeded to insert the shell or case below
the coffin the head separated from the trunk, and
the whole body, with the exception of the bones,

crumbled into dust." What was left was rever-
ently placed in the shell and carefully deposited
in the mausoleum.

" Bonnie Jean," the poet's widow, died in 1834,
and, on the night before her body was placed in
the mausoleum, a party of gentlemen went to
the vault with a view of obtaining a cast of the
skull for phrenological purposes. One of the
party, Dr. Archibald Blacklock, made a report,
in which he said that the cranium was found in a
high state of preservation, and that some small
portions of black hair intermixed with gray were
observed while detaching some extraneous matter
from the occiput. The skull was taken to the
house of a Mr. Kerr, a plasterer, and a cast taken
from it. A few hours later it was replaced in the
vault. There it lay unmolested until 1857, when
Burns' eldest son was interred in the mausoleum.
The skull was then seen by several gentlemen, and
found to be still unimpaired. By them it was
placed in its case very carefully, and the whole
was enclosed in a casket filled with pitch, so that
the relic might be preserved for ages yet to come.

Several copies of the cast of the skull were taken.
One went to Mr. George Combe, the eminent
phrenologist, who carefully measured it and pronounced it one of the largest and best developed
heads he had ever seen. Another cast was secured
by Colonel Joseph Laing, of New York, an en-
thusiast on all that pertains to Burns, and it was

willingly loaned by him to Mr. Caverley for the purpose of aiding in making the Albany statue as perfect as possible.

AN EARLY AMERICAN ELEGY ON BURNS.

THE following elegy, just found in the course of searching for material for the "Bibliography of Burns," is of interest as being probably the first poetical tribute to the memory of our National Bard published in the United States, or, indeed, in all America. It appears in "The American Universal Magazine," vol. I., pp. 447-448, published in Philadelphia in 1797. The author, it will be observed, has made a curious slip in the date of the Poet's death. Kensington is now a suburban part of the city of Philadelphia. To the poem the editor has appended the following note :—" In the poetical department, particularly, our readers will not expect perfection ; as valuable purposes may be answered by inserting juvenile attempts, which, though not contemptible, might be improved by the previous correction of a judicious friend, or the advantages of maturer study and experience."

GEO. F. BLACK

AN ELEGY
TO THE MEMORY OF
MR. ROBERT BURNS,
THE CELEBRATED SCOTS POET,
WHO DIED MAY 8TH, 1796.

I.

As late I walk'd beneath the moon's pale rays,
  Accusing fortune of my scanty share,
How I had spent—mispent, my youthful days,
  To gain the favour of a venal fair ;
Instant a form, in solemn sable clad,
  Approach'd my path with heedless steps, and slow ;
Pale fading laurels hung adown her head,
  And her dishevel'd hair did indicate her woe.

II.

" Forbear," she cry'd, " nor think of woes but mine ;
  The pride of nature and these plains is dead.
The favourite songster of the tuneful nine,
  Is fled forever—Is forever fled,—
COILA'S my name—with BURNS I oft *did go*,
  And did his bold poetic flame inspire ;
Made his enraptur'd fancy smoothly flow,
  And taught the bard to catch from heaven the
    sacred fire.

III.

" With me he wander'd by the purling rill,
  With me he stray'd upon the distant lawn,
And oft we climb'd yon cloud-capp'd distant hill,
  And reach'd its summit by the early dawn.
O *Melpomene,* muse of tragic woe—
  Mourn him who sang of ruin and despair :
E'en smiling *Thalia,* fraught with sprightly glow,
  Lament his fate, who sung upon the banks of Ayr.

IV.

" Have we not seen him skim the dewy lawn ?
    And with advent'rous fingers sweep the lyre ?
Have we not seen him at the early dawn,
    Enraptur'd high with fancy's sacred fire ?
Has not his fame in distant lands been told ?
    Has not his voice been pleasant to our ear ?
Has not the youthful gay, the serious old,
    Been highly charm'd, who now must shed the bitter
        tear ?

V.

" Ye sportive Naiades of the gurgling rills,
    Lament his fate in *Irvine, Ayr*, and *Doon*,
Pour forth your plaints, till all the distant hills
    Do nod their sorrow to the silent moon :
For me, I'll weep while hills and streams endure ;
    I'll wand'ring mourn, and tell the groves my grief,
The lawn shall hear me at an early hour,
    Nor shall I ever deign to take the least relief.

VI.

" I go," she cry'd, " nor ever shall return—
    I go forever from this once lov'd field,
My fate is fix'd—disconsolate I'll mourn,
    Since Scotia now no longer charms can yield."
Her grief stung bosom heav'd with bitter sighs,
    She seem'd prepar'd to take her distant flight ;
She turn'd and left me with her tear-swol'n eyes,
    And in a cloud of mist evanish'd from my sight.

W. REID.

KENSINGTON, *February* 19, 1797.

BURNSIANA IN THE NEW YORK PUBLIC LIBRARY.

MR. JAMES LENOX (1800-1880), founder of the Lenox Library, now a part of the New York Public Library, as the son of a Scot, was much interested in Scottish history and literature. The last books purchased by him, acquired at sale of David Laing's library in December, 1879, comprised seven lots. These were all Burns items, namely :—(1) the 1786 Kilmarnock edition, which he acquired for £96 ; (2) the first Edinburgh edition, for which he paid £5 10s. ; (3) the two volume Edinburgh edition of 1797, which cost him only nineteen shillings ; (4) the enlarged Edinburgh edition of 1798, which cost him £4 4s. ; (5) the Poems and Songs ascribed to Burns, Glasgow, 1801, for which he paid £3 18s. ; (6) the Letters to Clarinda, 1802, at £3 12s. 6d. ; and (7) the Commonplace Book, 1872, at eight shillings.

Mr. Bernard Quaritch, the London bookseller, acted as his agent at the sale, and in the last letter from Mr. Lenox to him, Mr. Lenox refers to the purchases made at the sale, and then goes on to say : " For nearly a month I have not left my bed, and every exertion is extremely hurtful to me. I do not think I shall be able to make any further purchases of books. After the announcement in your letter, received this morning, of the purchase of the set of Burns' Works, our corres-

pondence, I fear, must cease. I cannot undertake
to write to you without injury to myself." The
letter is not in Mr. Lenox's hand, but is signed by
him. Mr. Lenox died on 17th February, 1880.

The copy of the 1786 Kilmarnock edition
contains two verses from the song " How lang and
dreary is the Night," in the autograph of the Poet.
There is also laid in a holograph letter from John
Gibson Lockhart to Dr. Laing, which reads as
follows :—

" SUSSEX PLACE, REGENT'S PARK,

April 12, 1851.

" Dear Mr. Laing,—I am very much obliged
to you for your Deloraine notes, albeit they leave
Mr. Croker's millstone what it was.

Your reminder anent Burns caused my cheeks
to burn. I had entirely forgotten how the book
came into my hands—but here it is, not, I hope,
injured beyond what a touch of the binder's skill
will repair.

Ever sincerely,

J. G. LOCKHART.

D. LAING, Esq."

The first Edinburgh edition is in the original
stiff blue paper boards.

The library also possesses two holograph letters
of the Poet, acquired at the Tite sale in 1874.
The first, dated Mauchline, 31st March, 1788, is
addressed to Mr. Robert Cleghorn ; and the second,

without date, is addressed to Clarinda. These
letters will be found in the Globe edition of Burns'
works, pp. 409-410, 546-547.

GEO. F. BLACK.

LIFE AND DEATH OF CUTTY SARK.

(From " LIFE OF ALLAN CUNNINGHAM," with
    Selections from his Works and Correspondence,
    by the Rev. David Hogg.)

THE real " Cutty Sark " was Katherine Steven,
or, as curtailed in the dialect of the district, Kate
Steen, by which she was commonly called, for no
one dared to address her by her *sobriquet*, through
fear of the sad consequences which might ensue.
She was born in a cottage near the Maidens, and
was brought up by her grandmother at Laighpark, in the parish of Kirkoswald, on the Carrick
shore, where she paid the debt of nature many
years ago, in a state of extreme indigence, when
she had attained a good old age, yet generally
dreaded to the last.

When Burns was attending Kirkoswald school
he was intimately acquainted with the dwellers
along the Turnberry coast. Shanter, the residence
of Tam ; Glenfit, the abode of " Souter Johnny ; "
and Laighpark were placed in the immediate
neighbourhood of each other, with other cottages
around, such as those of the miller and the smith.
Kate Steen and her " reverend granny " were

I

both well known to the Poet, and many an hour
he spent in their shieling, listening to the stories
of the withered beldame about pirates and smugglers,
and also spell-bound by the unconscious cantrips
of the young witch, Kate.

Saturday, in the Devil's calendar, was the
witches' Sabbath; and it is interesting to mark
the synchronical accuracy of the Poet in fixing
the time of the jubilant carousal—it was early on
Saturday morning. The market-day in Ayr being
then, as it still is, on Friday, the Carrick farmer
had sat " boozing at the nappy," till " the hour,
of night's black arch the keystane," when he
mounted his mare and took the road homeward.
By the time he reached Alloway Kirk the morning
was in and the orgies were begun.

The title of " Cutty Sark " was not an original
appellation of the Poet's invention, though it was
new in the use he made of it to the young wench
of Kirkoswald shore. In a letter to Captain
Grose, when collecting his " Antiquities of Scotland," he mentions three witch stories connected
with Alloway Kirk, in one of which there is an
account of a merry-making similar to that of his
own tale, or which was rather the foundation of
his tale, and when a belated farmer " was so
tickled that he involuntarily burst out with a loud
laugh, " Weel luppen, Maggie, wi' the short sark ! "
and, recollecting himself, instantly spurred his
horse to the top of his speed." In this, then,

we have the first idea of " Cutty Sark," and what was predicted of Maggie is happily converted into an appellation for Nanny.   But why Nanny ? There was doubtless the same reason for calling Kate Steen *Nanny* as for calling Douglas Graham *Tam*, and his wife, Helen M'Taggart, *Kate*—a desire to avoid the delicacy and the not over-agreeable consequences of direct personality.   But to return.

Kate Steen was universally acknowledged to be a woman of very industrious habits, and was of necessity frugal and economical of whatever she obtained.   She was accustomed, when travelling from house to house, to take her tow rock and spindle or twirling-pin with her, and spin as she went along.   Her kind and obliging disposition secured her a warm reception among the farmhouses in the neighbourhood, and she always returned to her shieling at Laighpark Kiln laden with an abundant supply of the common necessaries of life.   Her case was remarkable, but, we believe, by no means peculiar, in having the weird character forcibly thrust upon her.   She not only made no pretensions, but repudiated the idea, of being considered a witch ;   yet a witch she was held to be in public estimation, and in those days that was enough.   Her supposed insight into futurity and acquaintance with the destinies of men led also to the belief that she possessed a sway over fate from an intimate connection with Satanic

power. In after life the peculiarity of her dress
assisted in no small degree in investing her with
supernatural agency ; and, consequently, so much
was she dreaded by young and old that, whenever
she was espied on the highway afar off, with her
rock and tow, a different road was taken to avoid
coming in contact with her, as her presence produced great anxiety and fear, except when she was
known to be favourably disposed. Doubtless
she had the foibles and infirmities of her sex and
calling ; and it was, perhaps, not altogether
exaggeration when it was said that she was not
reluctant on certain occasions to tell, with an
ominous shake of the head, that her meal barrel
was nearly empty, and that kail and water made
but thin broth. Yet it was seldom this necessity
was pressed upon her ; for, whether from love or
fear, she received a seemingly cordial welcome,
and her departure for home gave her no cause to
suspect its truth. Still on some occasions the
complaint of Mause might have been hers :—

> " Hard luck, alake ! when poverty and eild,
>   Weeds out o' fashion, and a lonely bield,
>   Wi' a sma' cast o' wiles, should, in a twitch,
>   Gi'e ane the hatefu' name, ' A wrinkled witch.'
>   The fool imagines, as do mony sic,
>   That I'm a witch, in compact wi' ' Auld Nick.' "

Kate Steen was of *low* stature, even for a woman,

though we should infer differently from the description given of her as—

> " Ae handsome wench and walie,"

and also for the dexterous part she performed in de-tailing " noble Maggie " at the " keystane o' the brig." But Burns must be here considered as using a poet's licence, either for the sake of the rhyme, or to lend an additional grace to his heroine, even though a witch. A poet's *witches*, as well as his wenches, are oftentimes very exaggerated descriptions of humanity. Burns' lyric heroines, though adorned with the epithets," loveliest," " fairest," " bonniest," " sweetest," and " beyond compare," were, many of them after all, very mediocre specimens of the masterwork of nature. Nay, some of them, it is said, were scarcely up to what is generally regarded as the minimum standard of female beauty. So, in the description of " Cutty Sark," there is certainly much that is exaggerated, much intended to adorn the tale, though she was universally reported as in league with a certain dark conspirator. If not beautiful, she was doubtless powerful :—

> " For mony a beast to dead she shot,
>   And perished mony a bonny boat,
>   And shook baith muckle corn and beer,
>   And kept the country-side in fear."

Among the cantrips imputed to Kate Steen in

the above list is one which is but imperfectly un-
derstood, if known at all, in the present day,
" Mony a beast to dead she shot." What was the
" shoot of dead ? " It was a curse or denuncia-
tion of evil upon a living object, that bodily disease
and death might speedily overtake it. And it
was the popular belief in former days that if such
an imprecation were made by any one, and especially by one reputed " no canny," it could not fail
in producing the desired effect."

In the Kirk-session records of the parish of
Tinwald, Dumfriesshire, of date August, 1699, we
find that the " shoot of dead " was a crime demand-
ing more than ordinary church censure and dis-
cipline. A report having been laid before the
Session that "John Carruthers and Jean Wilson
were scolding together, and that the said Jean
did imprecate him and his beasts," they were cited
to appear at next meeting, which they did accordingly, but " John declared it was not Jean Wilson
(who was brought up by another party on a like
charge), but Bessie Kennedy, who, upon a certain
Sabbath, did wish that his horse might *shoot to
dead*—whereupon it fell sick, and he, bringing it
home, and, sitting at his house reading, the said
Bessie Kennedy came by, and he telling her that
his horse had not thriven since she cursed it, she
wished that the *shoot of dead* might light on him
and it both." Bessie was summoned, and denied
the charge, but acknowledged that when he told

her his horse had eaten none since she cursed it, she replied that if the *shoot of dead* should come on him too, he might give her the blame. Bessie was found to have behaved unchristianly, was rebuked for the same, and dismissed after promising greater watchfulness for the future.

But witches, notwithstanding their cantrips and charms and incantations, are not invulnerable to the shafts of death; and, however often they may have whidded over the green knowes, in the form of some sturdy grey maukin', with shot after shot rattling in the rear, when death draws the trigger the aim is sure. So the time came when "Cutty's" mortal career drew to a close; and the presentiment she had of the day and hour of her decease contributed not a little to confirm the popular reputation of her weird character. One morning she sent for one of her neighbours, and addressed him in the following terms :— " Noo, John, this is my hinmost day in this warl, and the mid-day hour and me will hae an unco struggle. Ye hae lang befriended me and mine, when few cared little how ill we fared. There's my meal barrel in the corner by ; mony a time ye hae filled it, but I shall need it nae mair. Tak' it as a present, along with the bake-brod and the bread-roller on the tap o't; and when I'm gane ye'll fin' a bottle in the cupboard, wi' some bread and cheese in the same place. Mak' yersel's comfortable, and mourn na for me."

The meal barrel was a twenty-pint cask, which had seen considerable service of a different kind; the baking-board was a few staves of a similar vessel nailed together; and the bread-roller was a long-necked brandy bottle. Such were the humble gifts conveyed in the dying bequest of " Cutty Stark," and they were till lately in the possession of her friend John, who has followed his grateful neighbour over the unrepassable bourne, and who presented these relics of a wondrous character as a legacy to our informant.

One by one the morning hours crept wearily away, and, exactly at the predicted time, the lingering spirit of " Cutty Sark " departed to another scene. After the necessary obsequies had been performed by some female neighbours to the lifeless body, and the curtains had been drawn closely around, they sat down before the fire to refresh themselves, as directed, with the comforts of the cupboard, when, lo ! ere the first morsel had been tasted or the cork drawn, down went the hearth and all upon it, while the whole party fled in terror to the door. After the consternation had been somewhat abated, one bolder than the rest ventured to look through the keyhole, in the fear lest another Alloway Kirk scene should be going on, but all was silent. With trembling hand she lifted the latch and looked in. The body was lying still in death upon the bed as when they left it, and the hearthstone had disappeared save a single corner. They all returned, and found that the cause of their terror was a large vault underneath the hearth, which had been used for the concealment of illicit spirits and other smuggled goods, and also for hiding renegades from the hands of justice. The stone had slidden off one of its end supports, and, with its superincumbent load, was precipitated below. With considerable difficulty the stone was raised and set with earth from an adjoining field ! the door was securely fastened, and a few days after the mortal remains of " Cutty Sark " were committed to the dust.

BURNS' LOVE FOR HIS WIFE.

" BURNS has been hotly assailed," writes Arthur Warren, in presenting "The Other Side of Robert Burns " in the *Ladies' Home Journal*, " because of his alleged indifference to his wife (Jean Armour), but the fact is he was ardently fond of her. Jean was true to him, and his true affection never really turned from her. Jean worshipped him—literally worshipped him. And when we study her devoted life we must agree that there must have been much that was admirable in the character of a man who was adored by so true a woman. Burns' biographers have paid too scanty attention to all this. There is no use in apologising for the defects of Bobbie's life, but there is such a thing as insisting

too heavily upon them. . . . Too much has been
made in the thousand stories of Burns' life of the
' Highland Mary ' episode, and too little of what he
really felt for Jean Armour, and of Jean's intense
loyalty to him and devoted care of him. The
real facts about Highland Mary will never be known.
They comprise the one episode of Burns' life which
is veiled in mystery. But one can study the Poet's
life closely enough to see that the persecution which
in the early days seemed to hopelessly separate him
from love drove him to Highland Mary for solace,
and that Mary's sudden death idealised that
Highland lassie in his memory. There was not
much more to it, and Jean never troubled herself
about it. There has been a sad waste of popular
sympathy over Highland Mary. It is to loyal
Jean our thoughts should turn. Burns' love for
her and for his children was very great. When
young, she must have been a handsome, comely
woman, if not indeed a beauty, and up to middle
life her jet black eyes were clear and sparkling.
Her carriage was easy, and her step light. In
ballad poetry her taste was good, and range of
reading rather extensive. Her memory, too, was
strong, and she could quote, when she chose, at
considerable length and with great aptitude. Of
these powers the Bard was so well aware that he
read to her almost every piece he composed, and
was not ashamed to own that he had profited by
her judgment.''

EARLY REVIEWS OF BURNS' POEMS.

THE *New London Magazine,* in the very year in which the first edition of Burns was published, has the following appreciative critique :—

"We do not recollect to have ever met with a more signal instance of true and uncultivated genius than in the author of these poems. His occupation is that of a common ploughman, and his life has hitherto been spent in struggling with poverty. But all the rigours of fortune have not been able to repress the frequent efforts of his lively and vigorous imagination. Some of these poems are of a serious cast, but the strain which seems most natural to the author is the sportive and humorous. It is to be regretted that the Scottish dialect, in which these poems are written, must obscure the native beauties with which they appear to abound, and renders the same unintelligible to an English reader. Should it, however, prove true that the author has been taken under the patronage of a great lady in Scotland, and that a celebrated professor has interested himself in the cultivation of his talents, there is reason to hope that his distinguished genius may yet be exerted in such a manner as to afford more generous delight. In the meantime we must admire the genuine enthusiasm of his untutored muse, and bestow the tribute of just applause on one whose name will be transmitted to posterity with honour."

The *New Town and Country Magazine*, of date August, 1787, speaks of him as follows :—

" Robert Burns, we are informed, is a ploughman, but blessed by Nature with a powerful genius. His subjects are not, as might have been expected, confined to the objects which surrounded him ; he is satirical as well as pastoral, and humorous as well as pathetic. These poems being " chiefly in the Scottish dialect," it must necessarily confine their beauties to a small circle of readers ; however, the author has given good specimens of his skill in English. The following stanza is not only very elegant, but highly poetical."

The stanza quoted is the ninth of the Cottar's Saturday Night, beginning :—

" Oh happy love ! where love like this is found."

It is marvellous that such true though somewhat stinted praise was given in that " elegant " age to one like Burns, whose mission was to abolish the shamming and affected style of poetry then accepted as the only recognised standard.

In the *Northern Gazette*, published in Aberdeen, several articles and quotations from the poems appeared in 1787, all breathing the same spirit of appreciation and generous praise. In this journal Skinner published a poetical epistle to Robert Burns before it became defunct in 1787. In literary circles, his worth was even then known.

It took longer to permeate the multitude. His death, however, did not create the feeling : it merely brought it to the surface and forced its expression.

ROBERT BURNS ON HIS DEATHBED.

LIFE'S day draws near the gloaming,
   The weary darg o't's dune,
And a' its dear delusions
   I maun relinquish sune ;
Sune will auld Mither Scotland
   The bard that lo'es her tyne,
And hear her loves and praises sung
   By ither tongues than mine.

Land o' the sturdy thistle,
   And winsome heather bell,
Thou wants nae quivering minstrel
   Thy pith and pride to tell ;
But strong within his bosom
   The tide of song should flow
Who dares to voice thy doughty deeds
   And dreams of long ago !

So well'd in mine the music
   That broke in waves of fire,
When in the flush of manhood
   I swept the patriot-lyre ;
And though my failing fingers
   Now feebler echoes wake,
Fain would their hinmaist effort be
   For dear auld Scotland's sake.

*   *   *   *   *   *   *

K

O dinna steek that shutter,
　And keep the licht awa' ;
But owre me in its glory
　Let ilka sunbeam fa' !
For in the mirksome chamber
　Where I sae sune maun be,
The bonnie heartsome Simmer Sun
　Will shine nae mair for me.

Blithe hae I been to see him
　Come owre the hills at morn,
Or in the e'enin', gildin'
　Wi' liquid gow'd the corn ;
When 'neath his bauld caresses
　Dame Nature beam'd wi' joy,
And ilka thing that breath'd was glad,
　And nane mair glad than I.

Then, rapt in poet ardour,
　Enchanted ground I trod,
As in my heart, sweet singin',
　I heard the voice of God ;
His warks were a' aboot me,
　I sang whate'er I saw,
For man and beast, and flower and stream,
　I lo'ed them, ane an' a' !

Noo, like a wauf o' Winter
　That comes afore its time,
The warld's breath has chilled me,
　And killed me in my prime ;
Dark clouds obscure the visions,
　Gar'd a' my being thrill,
And in my cauld and flutterin' breist
　The heavenly voice is still.

O' talents lichtly cared for,
 And noo ayont reca',
How, like a reckless spendthrift,
 I've cuist my wraith awa' !
What can I gi'e for answer
 When the dread Voice I hear
That o' my thriftless stewardship
 In thunder-tones'll speir ?

 * * * * * * * *

*Sweet lass, whase step, like music,
 Slips the lown chamber thro',
Whase touch is like an angel's
 Upon my burnin' broo—
O, frae the paths of virtue
 Ne'er let that fitstep stray,
And for a heavenly licht to guide
 This heart will ever pray.

And bairns—my blessings on ye !
 You'll sune be left your lane,
Wi' life's sair darg afore ye—
 In God's name—act like Men !
Abune a' fame or fortune
 For this my bosom yearns,
That man for honest worth should prize
 The sons of Robert Burns !

 * * * * * * * *

Dear Jean, the nicht grows eerie,
 I wat I'll slumber sune ;
O lay your loof in mine, luve,
 As ye sae aft hae dune ;
And on that faithfu' bosom
 Let this worn cheek recline,
That for a heart-beat I may pree
 The raptures o' lang syne.

* Miss Jessy Lewars.

O bonnie was the burn side,
  And fair the sylvan scene,
Where, 'neath the budding hawthorn,
  I trysted wi' my Jean ;
And as I fondly clasped her—
  A bliss beyond compare—
I trow the munelicht never shone
  On sich a happy pair.

Sinsyne, I've tried her sairly,
  But good and true she's been ;
And for a' that's come and gane yet
  She's still my Bonnie Jean !
There's nane in a' braid Scotland
  That's half sae dear to me ,
And ne'er a hand but this dear hand
  Shall close my weary e'e.

Then fare ye weel, my ain Jean,
  My first joe and my last,
Through ilka neuk in Scotland
  Our names entwin'd ha'e pass'd ;
And think na that she slichts us,
  Or sune forgot we'll be—
A hunder year will but increase
  Her pride in you and me !

But now on Life's illusions
  Maun close these e'en o' mine,
And to the Fount it sprang frae
  My soul I maun resign ;
Great Being ! in whose presence
  Ere morning I may stand,
Reach from the dark, to guide me through,
  Thine everlasting hand !

"THE LASS O' BALLOCHMYLE."

IN looking over some of Burns' poems, and lingering over some of the subjects of his love songs,
which are always a delight, and make a winter's
evening pass away all too quickly, it was easy to
be arrested by the beautiful song of "The Lass
o' Ballochmyle," beginning with

> " 'Twas even—the dewy fields were green,
>   On every blade the pearls hang."

Its intrinsic sweetness brought back a crowd
of touching memories, among them the thought
that it was the favourite song of the late James
Thaw, and sung by him with a charming simplicity
of style which will be long remembered by his
brither Scots in New York.

It's a song that sends one away back to Mauchline, that picturesque and breezy upland Ayrshire
village where the writer enjoyed many a happy
ramble.

> " Still o'er these scenes my memory wakes
>   And fondly broods with wiser care !
> Time but the impression stronger makes,
>   As streams their channels deeper wear."

Burns must have presented quite a figure in
those days in that district ; as " Rob Mossgiel "
he had already made himself known as a poet,
and as the principal factor in an intensely interesting love drama.   He had written to David Bryce,

at Glasgow, " You will have heard that I am going
to commence poet in print ; and to-morrow my
works go to the press.   I expect it will be a volume
of about 200 pages; it is just the last foolish thing
I intend to do ; and then turn a wise man as soon
as possible."   The world knows now how that
Kilmarnock edition was received, whose title-page
bore the words :—

" The Simple Bard, unbroke by rules of Art,
   He pours the wild effusions of the heart,
   And if inspir'd, 'tis Nature's pow'rs inspire,
   Hers all the melting thrill, and hers the kindly fire.—
                        Anonymous."

At the age of 27 he was still the rustic bard to some
extent, and in writing this song, in honour of Miss
Alexander of Ballochmyle, he was quite sensible
of his powers, but the lady being in another station
of life he had doubts as to using the poem in print.
" Had she been a country maid," or a Mauchline
belle, like any of the following, he might not have
been so particular—

" *Miss Miller* is fine, *Miss Markland's* divine,
   Miss Smith she has wit, and Miss Betty is braw ;
There's beauty and fortune to get wi' *Miss Morton ;*
   But *Armour's* the jewel for me o' them a',"

so he applied to the heroine of the song for her
permission to print it in his proposed new edition,
and he even begged Mrs. Stewart of Stair to use

her influence with Miss Alexander to that effect. When in Edinburgh, too, he complained, in a letter to Gavin Hamilton, that this song, along with another having a celebrated lady for its subject, were tried by a jury of *literati*, and the author forbidden to print them. He adds :—" I cannot help shedding a tear to the memory of two songs that have cost me some pains ; but I must submit. . . . My poor unfortunate songs come again across my memory. D—— the pedant, frigid soul of criticism for ever and ever ! "

In his letter to Miss Alexander the Poet describes with great minuteness the scene and the occasion which gave birth to the song, and refers to " the hoary hawthorn twig that shot across the way," to the " harmony poured forth by the feathered warblers," and to " the gaiety of the vernal year." The spot of meeting is now marked by a rustic grotto, in which a tablet is inserted, containing a *fac simile* of the Poet's manuscript of two verses of the song.

Dr. Robert Chambers, while on a visit to the Land of Burns collecting information, met many of the people who had known the Poet, or his immediate relatives and friends. And he has recorded, under date "Ayr, Monday, October 9th, 1837 :—Called upon Miss Alexander of Balloch-myle. Fine-looking old lady of 82. [She must have been 31 when the muse of Burns hailed her as the perfection of Nature's works.] Woman of

superior intellect and the finest natural character,
unaffected, old-fashioned manners. Story is that
she walked out after dinner along the brae behind
the house, when suddenly she came upon a man
who was standing musing. Startled by the unex-
pectedness of seeing a stranger in such a place in
dusk of evening, passed on without more than
looking at the stranger, whose personal appearance
was not very prepossessing. Burns was supposed
to have been on his return from ——, where he had
been fishing. He was taking a short cut, and was
trespassing. Some months later Miss Alexander
received the letter, which concluded by mentioning
that he wished to print it in the second edition of
his poems, but would not do so without her permission. She, knowing nothing of him but that
he was a village poet of indifferent character, did
not think proper to take any notice of it. A grotto
is erected at the place of meeting as near as she
could recollect. Miss Alexander uses rouge, and
probably used it when young, too. Droll to think
of the share this might have had in exciting Burns'
admiration. Wilhelmina Alexander died unmarried at Glasgow in 1843, at the age of eighty-
nine.''

It is interesting to note that the other song
having a celebrated lady for its subject was that
most popular of all his songs, '' Ye banks and braes
o' bonnie Doon.'' She was (according to Mrs.
Begg's memoranda) Miss Peggy Kennedy, a niece

of Mrs. Gavin Hamilton of Mauchline. Although born heiress of a considerable estate in Carrick—to which she ultimately succeeded—she, at the tender age of 17, proved herself to be one of many frail daughters of Eve who have loved " not wisely, but too well." Cunningham tells us that " this beautiful and accomplished woman fell a victim to her passion for M'Dougall of Logan." It was about the " time of the poet leaving Ayrshire for Edinburgh, at the close of autumn, 1786, that the sad story of this hapless daughter of beauty began to be talked of ; and ere he reached the Metropolis he seems to have composed, in reference to her fate, his never dying lyric, " Ye banks and braes o' bonnie Doon."

In this way the student of Burns has an interesting link connecting two of his exquisite songs, the subjects of which, although so different, coming within the eye and scope of the poetic artist, was at once expressed in the most melodious words, a charming and bewitching quality which we also find in his delightful description of his ain bonnie Jean:

> " I see her in the dewy flowers,
>   I see her sweet and fair ;
> I hear her in the tunefu' birds,
>   Wi' music charm the air :
> There's not a bonnie flower that springs
>   By fountain, shaw, or green ;
> There's not a bonnie bird that sings
>   But minds me o' my Jean."
>   —JOHN S. MACNAB, New York.

BURNS AND FREEMASONRY.

BURNS, beyond question (says Hunter in his
" Lectures on Freemasonry ") derived considerable advantage from Masonry. It is evident,
from the statements which he has placed on record,
that it contributed greatly to his happiness in
admitting him into close and intimate fellowship
with the wise, intelligent, and social, and furnishing
him with opportunities for enjoying the " feast
of reason and the flow of soul " in the most rational
and ennobling manner. It presented him also
with one of the best fields that he could find for
the improvement of his mind and the display of
his talents. In no other society are all the members
treated with so much indulgence, and placed on a
footing of so much equality. In the Mason's
Lodge, merit and worth are sure to be appreciated,
and to meet with appreciation and respect. When
the young and humble ploughman of Lochlea
joined the Lodge of Tarbolton, he was still in a
great measure unnoticed and unknown ; but no
sooner did he receive the stamp of Freemasonry,
than he took his place with Sir John Whitefoord
of Ballochmyle, Jas. Dalrymple of Orangefield,
Sheriff Wallace of Ayr ; Gavin Hamilton, writer,
Mauchline ; John Ballantine, Provost of Ayr ;
Professor Dugald Stewart, of Catrine ; Dr. John
M'Kenzie of Mauchline ; William Parker, Kilmarnock ; and a whole host of Ayrshire worthies,

high and low. By coming in contact with these men his manners were refined, his intellectual energies stimulated, and his merits acknowledged and applauded. Nay, Wood, the tailor ; Manson, the publican ; Wilson, the schoolmaster ; Humphrey, the " noisy polemic ; " and all the meaner brethren, seem very soon to have discovered his high intellectual qualities, for they were not long in raising him to the second highest office in the Lodge—an office that caused him, on ordinary occasions, to occupy the master's chair, and perform the work of initiation. In the school of the Lodge, he must, in a great measure, have acquired that coolness of demeanour, that dignity of deportment, that fluency and propriety of expression, and that acquaintance with philosophy and humanity which so astounded and electrified the sages and nobles of Edinburgh, and made his advent in that capital one of the most remarkable incidents in literary history. Instead of a clownish, bashful, ignorant rustic, the most learned and exalted citizens found that he was able and ready to take his place by their side, and that, in everything in which intellect was concerned, he was in some respects their equal, and in others greatly their superior. Burns was principally indebted to Freemasonry for any little gleam of prosperity that shone on his earthly pilgrimage. It was the Freemasons of Ayrshire who invited him to their tables ; who furnished him with advice ; who read his productions into fame; and purchased and circulated the Kilmarnock edition of his poems. It was by the advice of his brother Mason, John Ballantine, of Ayr, to whom he inscribed his poem, entitled "The Brigs of Ayr," that he repaired to Edinburgh, and not, as is generally said, by the letter of Dr. Blacklock to the Rev. George Laurie of London, which says not one word of his coming to Edinburgh, but merely suggests the desirableness of publishing a second edition of his poems. His brother, Gilbert, expressly states that, when Mr. Ballantine heard that the Poet was prevented from publishing a second edition, from the want of money to pay for the paper, he "generously offered to accommodate Robert with what money he might need for this purpose (£27); but advised him to go to Edinburgh as the fittest place for publishing." When Burns, acting on this advice, set out for Edinburgh he had not, as he himself states, a single letter of introduction in his pocket, and we would be quite at a loss to know how he was able to form so sudden an acquaintance with the nobility and *literati* of the Scottish capital, were we not assured, on good authority, that he owed this, in a great measure, to his appearance among the Masonic brethren. It was they who introduced him into the best circles of society; who put money in his purse to supply his wants; who procured subscribers for the new edition of his poems; who formed his companions in his tours ; who were his chief epistolary correspondents; who gave him accommodation in their houses ; who obtained his appointment in the Excise ; and who, last of all, put him in possession of a farm— the chief object of his desire.

As Masons, we are proud that Robert Burns was enrolled in the ranks of our Order, and while we should strive to avoid the " thoughtless follies that laid him low and stained his name," we should at the same time endeavour to imitate his ardent zeal, his open and generous disposition, and his manly and lofty independence.

THE   KIRKOSWALD   PERIOD.

IT is little more than mentioned in the written memoirs of Burns, that the Poet spent his nine- teenth summer (1778) in the parish of Kirkoswald, in the southern and more primitive district of Ayrshire.   His father was at this time the tenant of the small farm of Lochlee, in the parish of Tarbolton, in the comparatively refined district of Kyle.   What seems to have suggested his going to Kirkoswald school was the connection of his mother with that parish.   She was the daughter of Gilbert Brown, farmer, of Craigenton, in this parochial division of Carrick, in which she had many friends still living, particularly a brother, Samuel Brown, who resided, in the mis- cellaneous capacity of farm-labourer, fisherman, and dealer in wool, at the farm-house of Ballochneil,

L

above a mile from the village of Kirkoswald.
This Brown, though not the farmer or guidman
of the place, was a person held to be in creditable
circumstances in a district where the distinction
between master and servant was, and still is, by
no means great.   His wife was the sister of Niven,
the tenant ;   and he lived in the " chamber," or
better portion of the farm-house, but was now a
widower.   It was with Brown that Burns lived
during his attendance at Kirkoswald school,
walking every morning to the village where the
little seminary of learning was situated, and
returning at night.

The district into which the young Poet was thus
thrown has many features of a remarkable kind,
Though situated on the shore of the Firth of Clyde.
where steamers are every hour to be seen on their
passage between enlightened and busy cities, it is
to this day the seat of simple and patriarchal
usages.   Its land, composed of bleak green uplands,
partly cultivated and partly pastoral, was, at the
time alluded to occupied by a generation of
primitive small farmers, many of whom, while
preserving their native simplicity, had superadded
to it some of the irregular habits arising from a
concern in the trade of introducing contraband
goods on the Carrick coast.   This business was first
carried on there from the Isle of Man, and afterwards to a considerable extent from France,
Ostend, and Gottenburg.   Persons engaged in it

found it necessary to go abroad, and enter into business with foreign merchants ; and by dealing in tea, spirits, and silks, brought home to their families and friends the means of luxury and finery at the cheapest rate.   Such dealings did not prevent superstition from flourishing amongst them in a degree of vigour in which no district of lowland Scotland now presents any example.   The parish has six miles of sea-coast ; and the village, where the church and school were situated, is in a sheltered situation about a couple of miles inland.

The parish schoolmaster, Hugh Rodger, enjoyed great local fame as a teacher of mensuration and geometry, and was much employed as a practical land-surveyor.   On the day when Burns entered at the school, another youth, a little younger than himself, also entered.   This was a native of the neighbouring town of Maybole, who, having there completed a course of classical study, was now sent by his father, a respectable shopkeeper, to acquire arithmetic and mensuration under the famed mathematician of Kirkoswald.   It was then the custom, when pupils of their age entered at a school, to take the master to a tavern, and implement the engagement by treating him to some liquor.   Burns and the Maybole youth, accordingly, united to regale Rodger with a potation of ale, at a public-house in the village, kept by two gentlewomanly sort of persons named Kennedy— Jean and Anne Kennedy—the former of whom was destined to be afterwards married to immortal verse, under the appellation of *Kirkton Jean*— and whose house, in consideration of some pretensions to birth or style above the common, was always called " the Leddies' House." From that time, Burns and the Maybole youth became intimate friends, insomuch that during this summer neither had any companion with whom he was more frequently in company. Burns was only at the village during school hours ; but when his friend Willie returned to the paternal home on Saturday nights, the Poet would accompany him, and stay till it was time for both to come back to school on Monday morning. There was also an interval between the morning and afternoon meetings of the school, which the two youths used to spend together. Instead of amusing themselves with ball or any other sport, like the rest of the scholars, they would take a walk by themselves in the outskirts of the village, and converse on subjects calculated to improve their minds. Both attained eminence : the one became the most illustrious poet' of his country ; and it is not unworthy of being mentioned in the same sentence, that the other advanced, through a career of successful industry in his native town, to the possession of a large estate in its neighbourhood, and some share of the honours usually reserved in this country for birth and aristocratic connection.

The coast in the neighbourhood of Burns'

residence at Ballochneil presented a range of rustic
characters upon whom his genius was destined to
confer an extraordinary interest. At the farm of
Shanter, on a slope overlooking the shore, not far
from Turnberry Castle, lived Douglas Graham, a
stout, hearty specimen of the Carrick farmer, a
little addicted to smuggling, but withal a worthy
and upright member of society, and a kind-natured
man. He had a wife named Helen M'Taggart,
who was unusually addicted to superstitious
beliefs and fears. The *steading* where this good
couple lived is now no more, for the farm has been
divided for the increase of two others in its neighbourhood ; but genius has given them a perennial
existence in the tale of Tam o' Shanter, where
their characters are exactly delineated under the
respective appellations of Tam and Kate. At
Glenfit, near Shanter, there was a shoemaker
named John Davidson, whose wife, Ann Gillespie,
had acted as nurse to the mother of Burns, on which
account there was always a friendship between the
two families. In the language of a local poet,
John

——was a gash wee fodgel body,
Stood on his shanks baith tight and steady,
As gleg's a hawk, as tough's a widdy ;
　　Had gabby skill
To crack a joke wi' wit aye ready,
　　Out-owre a gill.

We are informed by the same authority that, at
Damhouse, likewise near Shanter, close by the

shore, lived Hugh Brown, a miller, and also Jock
Niven, a blacksmith, two drouthy neighbours, to
whom the well-known lines are applicable—

> That, ilka medler wi' the miller,
> Thou sat as lang as thou had siller ;
> That, every naig was ca'd a shoe on,
> The smith and thee got roaring fou on.

Living so near each other, and partaking of the
same tastes, it was impossible that the four Carrick
men here described should not have been endeared
friends. What says our Maybole Poet on this
point ?—

> Near neighbourhood right weel assisted,
> To souther friendship that consisted
> In drinking jorums, when they listed
>   Their placks to jingle ;
> In ae short mile ilk might ha'e rested
>   At ither's ingle.
>
> Gaun to the kirk, they whiles foregather'd,
> And, warslin' sair wi' conscience, swither'd,
> Till wi' o'ercoming drouth sair bother'd.
>   The bell's last croon
> Gat them in Kirkton Jean's fast tether'd,
>   A' snugly doon.

There, we suppose, to drink till Monday.

Graham dealt extensively in malt, which he
supplied not only to many of the neighbouring
hostelries, but also to some of the taverns in Ayr.

It was his business to go there once-a-week—on Friday, which was the market-day of the burgh. His friend Davidson, dabbling a little in the business of a tanner, had wares to dispose of and money to gather on the same day and in the same place ; so the two would proceed to town together. As Graham had to call for liquor at every customer's house, by way of showing respect and gratitude, he had much more of that commodity at his disposal than he chose to make use of himself ; and he was accordingly very glad when the Souter or any other friend went in with him to partake of it. In riding home late one night in the midst of a dreadful storm, Graham lost his bonnet, which contained his purse, and when he arrived at Shanter, could see no better means of excusing the circumstance to his superstitious wife than to state that it had been taken from him by a troop of witches and warlocks whom he had disturbed at their midnight orgies in Alloway Kirk.   He afterwards found his bonnet in a place near the wayside, and the money within it ; but the tale by which he had imposed on his wife was not forgotten.

One day, when the scholars of Kirkoswald had been favoured with a holiday, Burns went upon a fishing excursion with a few of the natives, including John Niven, the son of Mr. Niven of Ballochneil, and his own bedfellow.   While they were out at sea, the wind rose, and gave token of an approaching tempest, which made the company very

uneasy, and alarmed even the men who were
accustomed to fish those seas. The young Poet
rallied them on their fears, and said he was willing
to stay where he was while it blew off shore,
although it should "blaw the horns aff the kye."
They made nevertheless for the coast, and landed
at the Maiden Heads, two large rocks which rise
upon the beach at the farm of Shanter. As they
proceeded homeward, the storm rose to its height,
accompanied by thunder and deluges of rain.
They therefore took shelter in Shanter farm-house,
where they found that the guidman was absent at
Ayr market. Kate received them frankly, and
in course of conversation launched forth into a
lament about the habits of her husband, his
toping with the miller, smith, and souter, and his
late hame-comings from market, prophesying that

> ——" late or soon,
> He wad be found deep drowned in Doon."

Amongst other things, she spoke of Alloway Kirk,
which she said he dreaded to pass at night, and
yet he never on that account took care to come
home an hour earlier. The Poet and his friends
stayed with her till twelve o'clock, and then left
her still waiting, "a waefu' woman," for the return
of her husband.

It was probably some time after this that the
affair of the bonnet took place. The story having
got abroad occasioned much amusement, and

Graham, wherever he went, was rallied about his adventure at Alloway Kirk. The people of the district who were engaged in the contraband trade had a quarterly meeting for the arrangement of their accounts, and at these meetings there was usually much conviviality. At one, which took place during Burns' residence in the country, he and the goodman of Shanter were brought together, and the latter was rallied most unmercifully by his friends about the story of the bonnet, the whole of which was minutely inquired into and made a subject of mirth. Thus was the youthful Poet supplied with the best possible commentary upon what he had heard from Kate's own lips about her husband's practices. It is not to be doubted, we think, that the circumstances and traits of life and character which on these two occasions came under his notice were what supplied him with the materials of his inimitable tale of diablerie. Yet it is curious to learn from the tradition of the district, that the young Poet who was now studying mankind with so much assiduity, and no doubt secretly delighting himself with the comic points of the characters of his compeers, was afterwards reported by those very compeers to have always appeared to them a heavy, sulky sort of fellow. Youthful inexperience had probably made him silent amidst their boisterous talk, and we know well that, when not in the act of speaking, his countenance was sombre. Little did they imagine that under that dark brow resided powers fitted to make the whole world party to their mirth.

At Ballochneil, Burns engaged heartily in the sports of leaping, dancing, wrestling, throwing the stone, and others of the like kind. His innate thirst for distinction and superiority was manifested in these as in more important affairs ; but though he was possessed of great strength, as well as skill, he could never match his young bed-fellow, John Niven. Obliged at last to acknowledge himself beaten by this person in bodily warfare, he had recourse, for amends, to a spiritual mode of contention, and would engage young Niven in an argument about some speculative question, when, of course, he invariably floored his antagonist. His satisfaction on these occasions is said to have been extreme. One day, as he was walking slowly along the street of the village in a manner customary to him, with his eyes bent on the ground, he was met by the Misses Biggar, the daughters of the parish pastor. He would have passed without noticing them if one of the young ladies had not called him by name. She then rallied him on his inattention to the fair sex, in preferring to look towards the inanimate ground, instead of seizing the opportunity afforded him of indulging in the most invaluable privilege of man, that of beholding and conversing with the ladies. " Madam," said he, " it is a natural and right thing for man to contemplate the ground, from whence *he* was taken, and for woman to look upon and observe man, from whom she was taken." This was a conceit ; but it was the conceit of no vulgar boy.

At his departure from Kirkoswald, Burns engaged his Maybole friend and some other lads to keep up a correspondence with him. His object in doing so, as we may gather from his own narrative, was to improve himself in composition. "I carried this whim so far," says he, "that, though I had not three farthings' worth of business in the world, yet almost every post brought me as many letters as if I had been a broad plodding son of day-book and ledger." To his Maybole friend, Willie, in particular, he wrote often, and in the most friendly and confidential terms. This correspondence continued till the period of the publication of the poems, when Burns wrote to request his friend's good offices in increasing his list of subscribers. The young man was then possessed of little influence ; but what little he had he exerted with all the zeal of friendship, and with considerable success. A parcel of copies was accordingly transmitted in proper time to his care, and soon after the Poet came to Maybole to receive the money. His friend collected a few choice spirits to meet him at the King's Arms Inn, and they spent a happy night together. Burns was on this occasion particularly elated, for Willie, in the midst of their conviviality, handed over to him above seven pounds, being the first considerable sum of money the poor bard had ever possessed. In the pride of his heart, next morning he determined that he should not walk home, and accordingly he hired from his host a certain poor hack mare, well-known along the whole road from Glasgow to Portpatrick—in all probability the first hired conveyance the Poet Burns had ever enjoyed, for even his subsequent journey to Edinburgh, auspicious as were the prospects under which it was undertaken, was performed on foot. Willie and a few other youths who had been in his company on the preceding night walked out of town before him, for the purpose of taking leave at a particular spot ; and, before he came up, they had prepared a few mock-heroic verses in which to express their farewell. When Burns rode up, accordingly, they saluted him in this formal manner, a little to his surprise. He thanked them, and instantly added, "What need of all this fine parade of verse ?   It would have been quite enough if you had said—

> " Here comes Burns
> On Rosinante ;
> She's d——d poor
> But he's d——d canty."

When these pleasantries had passed, the Maybole youths allowed their poetical friend to go on his way rejoicing.   Such is the story of Burns' early

life among the rough-living fishermen and smugglers
of Kirkoswald.

—*The Scottish Reader.*

BURNS' EARLY DAYS IN EDINBURGH.

WHERE in literature can the episode of Burns in
Edinburgh be matched ? In its splendours and
its glooms alike it is unique. He was at the nadir
of his fortunes in Mauchline in the harvest of 1786.
The Kilmarnock edition of his poems had been
published. This was his joy, and he had no other
then. He had given over his share of the farm of
Mossgiel to his brother. His cash was limited
to a few pounds, derived from profits on his poems.
Dr. Blacklock, the blind poet, upon whom Dr.
Johnson, when a visitor in Edinburgh in 1773,
" looked with reverence," after reading Burns'
book, wrote to the Rev. Dr. Lawrie, a local minister
and the Poet's friend, suggesting that Burns
should go to Edinburgh and seek a publisher there
for a second edition of his poems. His Jean
Armour was forbidden to him. Highland Mary
was dead. His little travelling box, half-way to
Greenock, was recalled. The project of emigra-
tion to Jamaica was abandoned. Borrowing a
pony from his patron, Dalrymple of Orangefield,
he rode to Edinburgh—150 miles—by stages.
Already the farmers on the road were his readers.

M

They lodged him on the journey. At one point a white sheet was hoisted on a fork from the top of a stack of hay for a signal to all the neighbourhood that Burns had arrived. He had small luggage, little money. In Edinburgh he obtained lodgings of a common sort with John Richmond, a clerk whom he had known in Ayrshire, in Baxter's Close in the Lawnmarket, a part of the old town that was then fast deteriorating towards a slum. His letters were dated merely from "Edinburgh," and correspondents were asked to address their communications for him to the "care of Mr. Creech, bookseller."

Burns immediately emerged in Edinburgh as the "lion" of the season. His introductions were effectual. He had held office in Tarbolton and Mauchline as a Freemason. A special meeting of the St. Andrews Lodge, Edinburgh, was convened to receive him, when he was "toasted" with exuberance of Scottish fervour over "the dram" as "Caledonia's Bard," and replied with painful nervousness in an excellent speech. Before leaving Ayrshire, he had dined with Professor Dugald Stewart at Catrine House, and met there Sir John Whitefoord and the Earl of Daer. These gentlemen were in Edinburgh, and their influence was at his service. Mr. Dalrymple, of Orangefield, introduced him to the Earl of Glencairn, also to the popular "Harry Erskine," leader then of the Scottish Bar. He carried a letter to Dr. Blacklock, who introduced him to Henry Mackenzie, author of " The Man of Feeling," and editor of a weekly periodical called the " Lounger." In the issue of this curious old miscellany for December 9, 1786—ten days after Burns had arrived—Mackenzie published, as from his own polished pen, the earliest review of any note that had appeared of the ploughman's volume. Mackenzie was himself the " Man of Feeling," the kindliest creature of them all in that brilliant circle of wits. Yet has posterity justified him in respect of the " Lounger's " praise of Burns. At the distance of 120 years, the article reads like an appreciation of January 25, 1709. " To repair," to read its closing passage, " the wrongs of suffering or neglected merit ; to call forth genius from the obscurity in which it has pined indignant, and place it where it may profit or delight the world—these are exertions which give to wealth an enviable superiority, to greatness and to patronage a laudable pride." Mackenzie's appeal to the throng of Maecenases then in Edinburgh was successful. Poor, distressed, anxious, solitary on the road to Edinburgh, the Poet had hummed to himself the quaint lines of an old popular ballad :

> As I cam o'er by Glenap,
> I met an aged woman,
> Who bade me keep up my heart,
> For the best o' my days were coming.

In his early weeks in Edinburgh it seemed as if this presentiment had already been realised.

Around Burns then lay the old picturesque Edinburgh of the eighteenth century. The brilliant society of the Scottish metropolis opened its arms to receive him with a rush and gush of hero worship. At first the hero, he soon became to his admirers of the aristocracy little better than a freak of human nature, to be stared at in amazement. Upon the imagination of Burns the new urban environment was subduing at the outset ; he reeled and staggered in the mind before he found his feet secure on this intoxicating historic ground. What he saw was the old Edinburgh of the boyhood of Sir Walter Scott. Families of quality then resided in the old town, and the new town beyond and around Princes Street was but straggling, shapeless, and inchoate. Among the people letters and art were in glorious bloom after long centuries of war's devastation. Reconciled to the Legislative Union with England of 1707— an event Burns regretted—the city had betaken itself to imitation of Anglican modes. The historians and rhetoricians and philosophers were transplanting English literature upon the Scottish soil. They composed in the English tongue ; they affected English—at least the majority of them did—in public address and in conversation. It was not more than forty years since the Stuart

Rebellion of 1745, but the Jacobites were dead or dying, and, in common with Burns,

> Whose ancestors, in days of yore,
> Thro' hostile ranks and ruin'd gaps
> Old Scotia's bloody lion bore,

they were for the Stuart kings only in romantic sentiment, Jacobites in a poetical sense alone. The vernacular poetry of Fergusson and Allan Ramsay was neglected ; the great English masters, Shakespeare, Milton, Dryden, Pope, were the oracles of the hour. The times in Scotland were ripe for the reassertion in an insular genius of the potencies of the vernacular contemplated as a dialect of the Anglo-Saxon tongue. That Burns glorified the Doric in his most fetching poems and songs was a point against him in the superfine commonplaces of literary criticism in which Dr. Blair and Dugald Stewart indulged. The Poet, through sheer force of originality, overcame this barrier. He commanded the praise of a united academic Edinburgh that discovered in him a nation's wonder, throbbing irresistibly in his conversation, not less than in his poetry.

"Illiterate ! "   An "illiterate " poet ! This was the attitude of much of the fashionable society that entertained Burns, and held him forth as the "lion " of the hour in that old, proud, brilliant Edinburgh.   His hosts had no more than the most superficial knowledge of the Poet, and Burns' great

dark eyes saw them all from within and without.
" When proud fortune's ebbing tide recedes," he
wrote to Mrs. Dunlop, " you will bear me witness
that, when my bubble of fame was at the highest,
I stood unintoxicated with the intoxicating cup
in my hand, looking forward with rueful resolve."
—*T. P.'s Weekly.*

AN ECHO OF THE 1896 CELEBRATIONS.

A HUNDRED years ago to-day Robert Burns died
in the Mill Vennel of Dumfries—a " broken man "
in a lowly house. Strange it is to think that of
all the Scotsmen of his age—an age filled with
illustrious and memorable figures—this ploughman-
poet turned Exciseman, who for years had been
on the shady side of fortune, should be he whom
his countrymen and the world most delight to
honour. It is through no mere passing whim of the
hour that the name of Burns is to-day uppermost
in the thoughts of his fellow Scots, and of all men
throughout the world who love and know the pure
voice of nature and the spirit of our common
humanity. It is a name that has stood the test
of a whole century, and never was it so strong to
conjure with as it is now. New editions of the
poems of Burns, new biographies of his life and
estimates of his genius and his character, pour
from the press. There are daily gatherings to
unveil statues, to lay the foundation-stones of

memorials, to take part in processions, and ban-
quetings, and speechmaking. His songs were
never so much on the lips and in the hearts of the
people as they are to-day, when the gulf of a
hundred years yawns between us and the c'ouded
close of that brilliant and too brief career ; and
never did admiration for the Poet and love and, one
may freely add, respect for the man stand higher
than they do at the celebration of the Centenary
of his death. If it be said that acknowledgments,
post-dated a whole century, are poor and too late
amends for the neglect and slights which Burns
suffered in his lifetime, it may be answered that
this is not the light in which he would himself
have regarded the full-hearted and universal
tribute that is being paid to his memory. Rarely
has one lived and written who took more hearty
and honest delight in giving pleasure and in winning
applause from his fellows than Robert Burns.
In his best moods—and we are bound to take him
at his best—he had none of the pride that apes
humility. He could take his own measure as
well as the measure of his brother men. He was
conscious of the mighty gift with which he had
been endowed, and he knew, if he did not always
apply his knowledge, that a spirit so fine should be
touched only to fine issues. He did not pule over
his wrongs and his grievances. No one—not even
the bitterest of his biographers—was more keenly
aware than he of the " thoughtless follies " and

the graver errors which helped to bring upon him his misfortunes. He confessed them, and lamented them so passionately that meaner and less open natures, taking him at his own word, and measuring him with their own puny yardstick, have judged him and spoken of him as a monster of iniquities. So far is he from this that it may be asserted that in some of the songs written in those declining years at Dumfries, when, according to the theory dear to the hearts of his censors, he was pursuing a course of mental and moral degradation, there will be found more of right instinct and healthy insight—to say nothing of genuine poetry—than could be extracted from a gross of the carping critics of his life and of his work.

To Burns it would have been exceeding great reward for the pain and lowliness and disappointment of his latter days to know that he was leaving to his country and to his fellow-men a legacy of song that has grown more precious with the years, and at the end of a century is accounted among the richest possessions ever bequeathed to a nation. But his country and the world, that now cannot say enough in his praise, have they no sense of sadness and regret even while celebrating the close of a hundred years during which they have enjoyed and rejoiced in the inheritance of the dead poet? Does no strain of remorse mingle with the celebration of the finale of the most brilliant and inspiring episode in Scottish song? Undoubtedly there does.

Great part of the passionate affection and
enthusiasm with which the memory of Burns is
kept in remembrance arises from the feeling that
in his lifetime he fell on evil tongues and evil times,
and that even his death did not end the misappre-
hensions and misrepresentations of which he was
the victim. He had given royally, even prodigally,
of the gifts with which he was endowed ; and the
world had barely yielded him enough to live upon,
and the " unco guid " had peeped and pried into
all his faults, which were many, and had not minds
and hearts big enough to perceive and acknowledge
that these were, for the most part, the faults of
his qualities. There is in the ardour of the Burns
celebrations, anniversary and centenary, something of this sense of doing penance and making
expiation for martyrdom and calumny. It is a
generous and a natural feeling which is nowise
to be reproved or discouraged. It is, indeed, the
most persistent and spontaneous piece of hero-
worship which survives in our time. The great
heart of Scotland and of the world at least has not
misheard and misjudged the man who spoke for
it and to it in living words—who was, at one and the
same time, the National Bard and the poet of
humanity. It is perhaps neither possible nor
desirable to separate the life and the character of
Burns from his work. So directly does the latter
flow from the former that his poems might be, and
have been, made the basis of his biography. But

time and the implanted human sense of what is true and beautiful in man and in nature have been purging the wheat from the chaff. At the end of a hundred years the process should be well nigh complete. It is known and acknowledged of men that Robert Burns was not only a marvellously gifted poet, but an inspiring and beneficent force in the national literature and in the national life, and that, through Scotland and the Scottish dialect, he has influenced for good the ends of the earth. He has helped to raise the dignity of labour, and to make the humblest fireside a sacred place—to give sweetness to song, and reasonableness to the controversies of the sects and the moralists. Not merely did he purify the stream of popular poetry ; he was, as one of his latest biographers, Mr. Gabriel Setoun, points out, the reformer, all unknown to it, of the Kirk itself. For this, and for his other services, they do well who hold Burns in perpetual honour and who commemorate his centenary both with feasting and with heart-searching.

To Scotland and to Scotsmen Burns and his genius and fate come home with more poignant meaning and power than to the world without. He is their poet before being the poet universal. They feel that they can penetrate and be penetrated by his words and thoughts more than the outsider who has not grown up on the same soil and in the same air as Burns. They owe him special gratitude in that he has preserved as classic for all time their familiar tongue, which without him might have been doomed like other dialects to obscurity. He has rescued much of the choicest of their old lyrical poetry from oblivion ; he has married the sweetest of their musical strains to immortal verse of his own. He has done as much as, if not more than, any other man to make their national traits and customs and character known and honoured the world over. It is not only right but inevitable that the beginning, the middle, and the end of the Burns Centenary celebrations should take place in Scottish soil; and it is peculiarly appropriate that the great function held at Dumfries to-day should have as the presiding presence a Scotsman and a student and admirer of Burns so distinguished as Lord Rosebery. But while his native country takes and will continue to hold the lead in singing the praises of the most brilliant of her sons, echoes of what is spoken at Irvine and Dumfries and Glasgow will doubtless come back to us from the ends of the earth. They will be repeated in many tongues, and the chord of human sympathy struck on the Burns Centenary, and sounding so loud and so far, may well seem to optimist ears as presage of the time when

> Man to man the warld o'er
> Shall brothers be for a' that.

Though so much has changed in Scotland and
in the world, and changed for the better, since
Robert Burns laid down the heavy burden of his
life at Dumfries in 1796, we have still, it may be
feared, a long way to travel to the age of the
" brotherhood of man."   But this at least may be
said, that the more the poet of the " Cottar's
Saturday Night" and "Tam o' Shanter" is
loved and studied, and the more clearly it is seen
and acknowledged among men that, instead of
being a sort of freak of nature—a bundle of passions
and foibles endowed with genius—he was satirist,
thinker, reformer, literary artist, and even prophet
of his race and time, the nearer will the approach
be to that " good time coming " which it was the
mission of the Poet to proclaim.

—*Glasgow Herald.*